D0872387

Holinshed's Chronicles

Twayne's English Authors Series

Arthur F. Kinney, Editor

University of Massachusetts, Amherst

TEAS 556

THE
First and second
volumes of Chronicles,
comprising

1 The description and historie of England,
2 The description and historie of Ireland,
3 The description and historie of Scotland:

First collected and published by Raphaell
Holinshed, William Harrison,
and others:

Now newlie augmented and continued
(with manifold matters of singular
note and worthie memorie)
to the yeare 1 5 8 6. by
John Hooker *alias* Vowell Gent.
and others.

With conuenient tables at
the end of these
volumes.

Historia placeant nostrates ac peregrina

TITLE PAGE TO VOLUME 1 OF RAPHAEL HOLINSHED'S *CHRONICLES OF ENGLAND, IRELAND, AND SCOTLAND,* 1587.

This item is reproduced by permission of The Huntington Library, San Marino, California.

Holinshed's Chronicles

Alison Taufer

California State University, Los Angeles

Twayne Publishers
New York

Twayne's English Author Series No. 556

Holinshed's Chronicles
Alison Taufer

Twayne Publishers
1633 Broadway
New York, NY 10019

Library of Congress Cataloging-in-Publication Data

Taufer, Alison.
    Holinshed's Chronicles / Alison Taufer.
        p.   cm. — (Twayne's English authors series ; TEAS 556)
    Includes bibliographical references and index.
    ISBN 0-8057-4581-5 (alk. paper)
    1. Holinshed, Raphael, d. 1580? Chronicles of England, Scotlande,
and Irelande.   2. Great Britain—History—Tudors, 1485–1603—
Historiography.   3. Great Britain—History—To 1485—
Historiography.   4. Historiography—England—History—16th century.
I. Title.   II. Series.
DA130.T38   1999
941—dc21   98-38404
                                                                CIP

This paper meets the requirements of ANSI/NISO Z3948-1992 (Permanence of Paper).

10 9 8 7 6 5 4 3 2

Printed in the United States of America

To Daniel and Marisa, who long have awaited the completion of "mommy's book."

Contents

Editor's Note

No contemporary work was more influential in the development of early modern England than Raphael Holinshed's *Chronicles of England, Ireland, and Scotland*, which attempted to give the merging nations a past, a present, and a predictable future; Shakespeare's history plays are only one well-known way in which it determined history and shaped the imagination of the time. But recent revisionary work demonstrates that more than a half-dozen authors contributed to a book that continued to be expanded and rewritten after Holinshed's death and that this apparently singular chronology of past events is actually an anthology of myth, legend, fable, verifiable incident, telling anecdote, and deliberate polemic by writers with different intentions, styles, and agendas. Alison Taufer's masterful disassembly of the work identifies the different authors and their contributions, often sharply opposed, sometimes incompatible, and not infrequently didactic, and shows how these strands were woven together in the edition of 1577 and then rewoven following the expurgations and tampering of censors for an edition of 1587 that made the work the official Tudor government's view of England. Her study traces the reliability of the sources of the various chroniclers, looks at their differences, demonstrates how they dramatically changed the definition of history, and discusses how the *Chronicles* have been adapted and employed from its own time to ours. This is a highly accessible and useful book for the scholar and newcomer alike.

Arthur F. Kinney

Preface

Holinshed's *Chronicles* and its accompanying criticism can be likened to the story of the blind men and the elephant. Because of its vast size, any approach to the *Chronicles* necessarily results in a limited portrait of the text. Most studies focus on the later English history or Shakespeare's use of the *Chronicles* as a source for his plays and then extrapolate a view of the entire work from these limited sections. The purpose of my study is to provide an overview of all areas of the *Chronicles,* a project that in its scope presents its own problems and restrictions. Nevertheless, it is my hope that in exposing the richness and variety of the *Chronicles,* this work will encourage closer study of those portions that have previously been ignored.

Because of its influence on Shakespeare's historical plays, many readers are aware of the *Chronicles* solely as an English history. This misunderstanding is further reinforced by the fact that most libraries' editions of Holinshed's *Chronicles* are abbreviated excerpts of only those portions of the text used by Shakespeare.[1] In reality, the *Chronicles* encompasses far more than English history. An anthropological treasure horde, it contains detailed descriptions of the history, daily lives, customs, beliefs, and traditions of Scotland and Ireland as well as England.

Over the years, criticism of Holinshed's *Chronicles* has resulted in some surprisingly contradictory conclusions about its purpose and its value as a historical document. It has been criticized as disorderly and undisciplined, a collection of varying and often contradictory sources, without focus or a point of view. As early as 1639, Peter Heylyn wrote in his *Microcosmos* of "Voluminous Holingshead . . . full of confusion and commisture of unworthy relations." F. J. Levy's *Tudor Historical Thought,* still considered the most authoritative work on the subject of Tudor historiography, dismisses the *Chronicles* for its lack of selectivity and of organization: "Holinshed was rarely satisfied with merely one source, and he was much given to comparing the various reports of the same incident. The difficulty is that he never elaborated any method for deciding which source had priority, which should be followed . . . For him all sources were equal in value . . . Obviously, none of this led to any historical scheme of selection, and so Holinshed's *Historie* demonstrated most fully the idea that history could be written by agglomeration."[2] While Levy faults the *Chronicles* for its lack of a grand narrative or a unified sense of direction, in one of the most recent and in-depth studies of the text, *Reading Holinshed's* Chronicles, Annabel Patterson maintains that in its supposed weaknesses lie the work's very strengths.[3] She argues that in its inclusiveness, the *Chronicles* functioned as a national archive that made available to all readers the complex character of the nation's history, enabling them to evaluate and critique that history through their own understanding of the texts' multiple sources (Patterson 1994, 7–8). Whereas Patterson sees the *Chronicles* as an act of subversion, a text constructed in opposition to official discourse, Cyndia Clegg argues that the 1587 edition, printed under royal privilege, was regarded by Elizabeth's government as a means of circulating a favorable domestic and international image.[4] These conflicting views underscore the text's plurality and the impossibility of arguing a single thesis that applies to the entirety of the work that is Holinshed's *Chronicles*.

Lack of accessibility as well as vastness of size limit widespread understanding of the *Chronicles*. Unless one has access to a rare-books collection, it is impossible to read Holinshed's *Chronicles* as it appeared in the sixteenth century. With the exception of a special edition of the 1577 "Irish Chronicles," edited by Liam Miller and Eileen Power and published by the Dolmen Press in 1979, no modern edition of the 1577 *Chronicles* exists.[5] The AMS reprint of the problematic 1807 Ellis edition, which reinserts all materials censored in the sixteenth-century publications, is the only complete modern edition of the 1587 *Chronicles* available today.[6] Consequently, in this study, I refer to the Dolmen edition for the "1577 Irish Chronicles," to the original 1577 edition only for those sections of the text not found in the 1587 edition, and to the AMS reprint for the rest of Holinshed's *Chronicles* so that readers will be able to locate citations easily.

When citing from the AMS reprint, I note the differences between the 1577 edition and the 1587 edition of the *Chronicles*. To subsume the earlier edition into the later one, without making distinctions between the two, is to present a misleading picture of the *Chronicles*. These are two distinct texts with two different general editors and therefore markedly different editorial viewpoints. For example, many of the elements for which Holinshed's *Chronicles* has been noted, such as the vociferous nationalism and Protestant zeal of the commentary and marginalia, or the practice of inserting extraneous material into an unrelated narrative, do not exist in the 1577 edition. Furthermore, the woodcuts that adorn the 1577 edition and offer a running commentary on the nature of history in their depictions of violence, bloodshed, rebellion, and submission were deleted from the 1587 edition, thus creating an aesthetically and interpretively different experience for the reader of the later text.

Acknowledgments

I would like to express my appreciation to those scholars whose work on Holinshed's *Chronicles* has informed my own, especially Anne Castanien, Cyndia Clegg, and Annabel Patterson. I thank Cyndia Clegg in particular for her invaluable advice and assistance on this project and Arthur Kinney for his encouragement and support. I am grateful to the Huntington Library in San Marino, California, for the use of its copy of the 1577 edition and various copies of the 1587 edition and for permission to reproduce the title page of the 1587 edition of Holinshed's *Chronicles*. I am also grateful to my own department for the generous financial help that it provided through the Katherine Carter Fund.

Last, my deepest thanks and gratitude to César Bertaud and Renée Pigeon, who were always available when I needed a supportive audience. I am indebted to them both for their love, enthusiasm, and patience.

Chronology

utors. Although John Hooker alias Vowell appears on the title page as editor, it is now believed that Abraham Fleming served as general editor.

The Privy Council sends a letter to the Archbishop of Canterbury on 1 February requesting "the staye of furder sale and uttering" of the new edition of Holinshed's *Chronicles* "until they shall be reviewed and reformyd." Portions of the 1587 updates of the Scottish and English histories are censored and the corrected volumes are issued.

Chapter One
A Collaborative Effort: The Individuals Behind Holinshed's *Chronicles*

Holinshed's *Chronicles* belongs to a historical tradition that traces its English origins back to the time of Alfred the Great but was still employed during the Elizabethan era. This tradition, referred to as the chronicle or chronicle history, was the dominant form of historical record for almost seven centuries. A loosely organized compilation of previously written histories, primary sources, and original documents, the chronicle history relied on time as its organizing element. Events were reported in the chronicle history as they occurred without regard to their ultimate historical significance. Because chronology alone determined the organization and presentation of information, national political events, natural disasters, domestic crimes, local anecdotes, supernatural phenomena, and anything else that appeared in the sources were uncritically incorporated into the chronicle history as events of equal importance. Inclusiveness was the aim of the chronicler, and he would often provide two or more conflicting accounts of the same event, leaving the reader to judge which one was true.

Although the chronicle history continued to play an important role in the late sixteenth century, as witnessed by the publication of Richard Grafton's *Chronicle* (1569), Holinshed's *Chronicles* (1577 and 1587), William Camden's *Britannia* (1586), and John Stow's numerous chronicles and annals, as a genre it was already experiencing its decline. The new humanist approach to history, with its emphasis on the state and its organization of history around the personality of the monarch, provided a methodology of selecting historical materials according to their perceived veracity and their importance to the topic at hand. The result was a unified and focused narrative with an emphasis on human character and motivation, as exemplified by Polydore Vergil's *Anglica Historia* (1534) and Thomas More's *History of Richard III*. The Reformation had also brought a new vision of history to England. The desire to find his-

torical justification for current religious practices led to the search for
information that would verify the authenticity of the ancient Church in
England as established by Joseph of Arimathea and deny the supremacy
of Rome. Sources were evaluated and included according to their ability
to support these claims.[1]

An interest in causation, the recognition of anachronism, and the
questioning of textual authority further influenced the writing of history
in late-sixteenth-century England. The explanation of divine providence
as the primary cause of historical events gradually gave way to an analysis based on human actions and their consequences. The recognition of
the past as distinctly different from the present was another Renaissance
historiographical development, and historians questioned the veracity of
long-accepted records based on the argument that these records contained language and references to objects unknown at their supposed
time of origin.[2] Although a number of the later-sixteenth-century English chroniclers, such as Stow and even Holinshed, demonstrated an
awareness of these developments in their recording of events, by the seventeenth century the chronicle history was dismissed as a hopelessly
archaic and useless genre of historical writing. For modern scholars,
however, the encyclopedic nature of the chronicle history, its refusal to
privilege aristocratic history over popular tradition, and even its inclusion of conflicting sources render it a fascinating archive of cultural history and folklore.

The last and most comprehensive of the Tudor chronicle histories,
Holinshed's *Chronicles,* despite its name, was the product of more than a
dozen men's efforts. The Strasbourg printer and publisher Reyner Wolfe
had originally designed the *Chronicles* as a universal history and cosmography. After his death in 1573, the publishers George Bishop, John Harrison, and Lucas Harrison took over the financing of the project; decided
to limit its scope to England, Scotland, and Ireland; and employed
Raphael Holinshed, Wolfe's research assistant, to finish it. Holinshed
edited the entire work and wrote the English and Scottish history, but
the "Description of England" and the "Description of Scotland" were
written by the historian and topographer William Harrison and the
"Description of Ireland" and the "Thirde Booke of the Historie of Ireland" were contributed by Richard Stanyhurst. The 1577 *Chronicles*
appeared in two lavishly illustrated folio volumes; the first included the
"Description of England" followed by the "Historie of England" before
the Norman conquest, the "Description of Scotland," the "Historie of
Scotland," and finally the "Description of Ireland" and the "Historie of

Ireland." The entire second volume continued the "Historie of England" from 1066 to Elizabeth's reign.

Although Holinshed had died in 1580, the success of the 1577 *Chronicles* led the two surviving publishers, Bishop and Harrison, to join with Ralph Newbery, Thomas Woodcock, and Henry Denham to prepare a revised and updated version of the text. John Hooker's name appears on the title page as editor, but recent scholarship has demonstrated that it is more likely that Abraham Fleming served as editor, indexer, and "learned corrector" of the 1587 edition, since Fleming's contributions appear throughout the text while Hooker's are mainly limited to the expansion and update of the "Historie of Ireland."[3] Francis Thynne updated the Scottish history, John Stow and Abraham Fleming updated the English history, and William Harrison, the only remaining member of the original team of writers, rearranged and expanded the "Description of England." The greatly augmented 1587 edition resulted in three folio volumes with numerous editorial modifications. The woodcuts of the 1577 edition were deleted, but elaborate indexes were added and the pagination was standardized. The entire second volume was devoted to Scotland and Ireland, but the Irish section, which appeared last in the first volume of the 1577 edition, was placed before the Scottish section. The history of England before the Norman Conquest was divided into books and then into chapters with detailed summary titles. Despite its lengthy and often tangential additions and its cumbersome size, the 1587 edition of the *Chronicles* also proved successful.

Raphael Holinshed

Raphael Holinshed, the author and editor whose name graces the title of the *Chronicles,* therefore played an important but relatively limited role in its production history. Holinshed contributed only to the edition of 1577 and died seven years before the 1587 revision and reissuance. Ironically, although this second edition of the *Chronicles* also carries his name, Holinshed did not work on the 1587 Holinshed's *Chronicles,* widely believed to be the edition that Shakespeare used and the one employed almost exclusively by scholars and editors over the last four centuries.

Little biographical material exists on Holinshed. His date of birth is unknown, but he is believed to have been the son of Ralph Holinshed or Hollinshed of Cophurst in the township of Sutton Downes, Cheshire. A member of the clergy, he appears to have matriculated from Christ's

College, Cambridge, in 1544. He served in the church for a time before being employed by the printer Reyner Wolfe as a translator and assistant for the universal cosmography that Wolfe spent the last 24 years of his life compiling. After Wolfe's death in 1573, a syndicate of three publishers, George Bishop, John Harrison, and Harrison's half-brother, Lucas Harrison, employed Holinshed to finish the cosmography in a far more abbreviated form. The work was now to include only England, Scotland, and Ireland, since Wolfe had already accumulated the greatest part of the materials for those countries. Holinshed edited the entire 1577 edition, but his authorial contributions are limited to the English, the Scottish, and the first section of the Irish histories. In his will dated 1 October 1578, Holinshed describes himself as a steward to Thomas Burdet of Bramcote, Warwickshire, to whom he left all his notes, books, and manuscripts. It is believed that he died at Bramcote in 1580.[4]

Reyner (or Reginald) Wolfe, to whom the *Chronicles* owes its origin, had at first conceived of the *Chronicles* as a universal history and cosmography, possibly based on the German Protestant model of a detailed historical study written to reveal God's will in this world.[5] Wolfe, a Strasbourg printer, was actively involved in Reformation politics. Personally invited by Archbishop Cranmer, he emigrated to England sometime before 1537. He later served Cranmer as an emissary to some of the major Continental Reformers of his day, annually visiting the Frankfurt fair and bearing letters on these visits from Cranmer to Martin Bucer, Heinrich Bullinger, and other Reformers and from Thomas Cromwell to English agents in Germany.

In addition to being involved in Reformation activities, Reyner Wolfe established himself as a pivotal figure in the publishing history of sixteenth-century England. By 1543 he had set up the first and only printing house known to have existed in Paul's Cross Churchyard and was printing, publishing, and selling books in a large property rented from the Bishop of London.[6] Edward VI granted him the positions of royal printer, king's bookseller, and king's stationer. He was the first to hold a patent as printer to the king in Latin, Greek, and Hebrew. Listed in the original charter granted by King Philip and Queen Mary to the Stationers' Company in 1554, he served as master of the company in 1559, 1564, 1567, and 1572.

Wolfe's interest in antiquities, like his interest in religion, manifested itself early in his English career. His first publications included the writings of Archbishop Cranmer as well as the work of the famous antiquarian John Leland. Before Leland's death in 1552, Wolfe acquired many of his manuscript collections for the *Universal History or Cosmography,* which the printer had started in 1548. By the time of his death in 1573, Wolfe had collected the bulk of his materials for the English, Scottish, and Irish sections and had employed Holinshed to work on the project under his direction, but he had completed nothing. Wolfe's manuscript collection, much of which had been acquired from Leland, was purchased in turn by the antiquarian John Stow. Stow used the manuscripts for his contributions to the 1587 Holinshed's *Chronicles* and for his own historical works. He also prepared from Wolfe's manuscripts a history of England that he entitled *Reyner Wolfe's Chronicles,* but it was never published because Stow died before he could send it to press.[7] Due to the diligence of his son-in-law John Harrison and his associates, Wolfe's project was spared a similar fate. The two Harrisons and Bishop, as Wolfe's executors and associates, decided to see the project through to completion, but in a decidedly scaled-down format with Raphael Holinshed, who had worked as Wolfe's assistant, serving as editor.

William Harrison

To assist Holinshed, William Harrison, topographer, chronologer, and historian, was brought on to the project to write the "Description of England" and to translate into English a description of Scotland derived from Hector Boece's *Scotorum Historiae* and John Bellenden's Scottish translation of that work. Harrison was the only member of the original group of writers also to work on the second edition of the *Chronicles.* His contribution to the 1587 *Chronicles* included a rearrangement and expansion of the "Description of England."

Harrison, whose religious point of view was probably the most radically Protestant of all the contributors to the *Chronicles,* had briefly flirted with Catholicism during Mary's rule, and his education reflects the shifting tides of religious belief in England under the various Tudor monarchs. He was born into a wealthy London merchant family in 1535, during Henry VIII's reign, and attended St. Paul's School, which was founded by Dean Colet and advocated the older, more conservative humanism of Thomas More and his circle. He attended Westminster School under the headmastership of the Reformer Alexander Nowell during Edward VI's reign. At Oxford, he attended Christ Church, which became a center of Catholic reaction during Mary's reign. In a brief Latin biography that appears on a blank leaf of Harrison's copy of John Bale's *Scriptorum illustrium majoris Britannie ... catalogus* (Basle,

1557–1559), Harrison's tenure at Oxford University, where he received his bachelor's degree in 1556 and his master's degree in 1560, is described in the following terms: "While at the university he flung himself into the filth of papistry and became a shaven worshipper of Baal; he completely deserted the Christ he had earlier known as well as his age permitted. But God in His mercy recalled him from this insanity shortly before Mary's death, after he had heard, secretly but with good effect, Cranmer, Ridley, Latimer, and other preachers of Christ. He would not, perhaps, have escaped harm if that Jezebel had reigned longer, whom the Almighty Father wonderfully carried off, together with Pole, to the solace of the whole church." George Edelen, Harrison's biographer, points out that it is difficult to take literally the assertion that Harrison heard the Oxford martyrs preach in secret, but the emphasis of this passage seems to be that Harrison did reconvert to Protestantism, in the face of personal danger, before Mary I's death.[8]

Most of Harrison's adult life was spent in the countryside, a fact that probably influenced his sympathetic account of the English rural population in his "Description of England." He was chaplain to Sir William Brooke, Lord Cobham, who gave him the rectory of Radwinter in Essex in February 1559, which he held until his death. He also held the vicarage of Wimbish in Essex from January 1571 to the autumn of 1581, which he obtained from Francis de la Wood.[9]

Harrison's hostility to the Catholicism that he had embraced in his youth permeates most of his writings, including the "Description of England." His position toward the Church of England remains more ambiguous, however. As Patterson has pointed out, the 1587 revision of the "Description" shows a definite shift in his attitude from the 1577 version. In the 1577 edition, despite his Puritan sympathies, Harrison worries over the "want of discipline in the church" and applauds Elizabeth I for her efforts to bring England into "a limited compass of uniformity." The 1587 "Description" contains a number of attacks on the English Church, including pointed criticism of the church's higher clergy, complaints over the economic status of the lower clergy, and approval of the church's decision to reduce church festivals to 27 from the 95 of Roman Catholicism. In fact, Harrison suggests an even greater reduction to three: Christmas, Easter, and Whitsun, a suggestion that would clearly mark him as a Reformer (Patterson, 1994, 58–70). Harrison also veered from the uniformity of Elizabeth's church in his advocacy of clerical marriage, which Elizabeth rejected. By 1571, he was married to Marion Isebrande, an act that does not seem to have affected his standing as a clergyman. He was appointed canon of Windsor in 1586 and died there in 1593.

Richard Stanyhurst

Richard Stanyhurst, the third contributor to the 1577 edition, was a member of a prominent Anglo-Irish family that had settled in Ireland in the fourteenth century. His great-grandfather and grandfather had been lord mayors of Dublin, and his father, James, was recorder of the city and speaker of the Irish House of Commons in the Parliaments of 1557, 1560, and 1568. Although born in Ireland, Stanyhurst attended University College, Oxford, from 1563 to 1568, where he became a pupil of Edmund Campion. After graduating, Stanyhurst studied law at the Inns of Court, but his interest in history and literature made him decide to return to Ireland in 1569 so that he could devote himself to Irish history and geography. Campion accompanied Richard to Ireland in hopes of directing a restored Dublin University, which James Stanyhurst and Henry Sidney, then lord deputy of Ireland, were attempting to resurrect. While residing with the Stanyhursts, Campion employed James's personal recollections as well as his collection of books and manuscripts to write his Irish history.[10] In turn, the younger Stanyhurst used Campion's history as a source for his contributions to Holinshed's *Chronicles*: "The Description of Ireland" and "The Thirde Booke of the Historie of Ireland," which covered Henry VIII's reign.

After his education in England and return to Ireland, Stanyhurst became schoolmaster to the children of Gerald Fitzgerald, the 11th earl of Kildare, the leading nobleman in the Pale at that time. During his tenure there, Stanyhurst was accused of plotting to smuggle Lord Garret, Gerald's son and his pupil, out of the country to Spain, where the young nobleman was to be married to King Philip II's daughter. Garret was then to return to Ireland as viceroy for the Spanish king. Although this was supposed to take place around 1573, Stanyhurst was not questioned about the incident until 1580, when he had already relocated to England. He was arrested in September of that year and examined. In November, Robert Beale, secretary to the Privy Council, reported to Leicester that he had investigated Stanyhurst's background and that a search of his London home for incriminating documents revealed nothing. Stanyhurst was then accused of and arrested for being involved in another plot in which several Catholics in Ireland and England allegedly conspired to bring Mary, Queen of Scots, to Munster, where an invasion of England was to be organized and the city of London raised in readiness by Hugh Offley, Giles Garton, Richard Stanyhurst, and others.[11]

Although the first plot was never proven and the second plot was later revealed to be a fiction, Stanyhurst's close friendship with Campion, who at the time was imprisoned for treason, as well as his earlier employment in the house of the Earl of Kildare, who was arrested in 1575 on suspicion of consorting with rebels, caused the government to continue to regard him with suspicion. This, along with the deaths of his wife, Janet, in childbirth in 1579 and his pupil Garret in 1580, and the impending execution of his mentor, Edmund Campion, for treason in December 1581, led Stanyhurst to emigrate to the Low Countries early in 1581 after he was released from prison. He never returned to England or Ireland.

After leaving England, Stanyhurst wrote two other Irish histories, both in Latin: *De rebus in Hibernia gestis* (Antwerp, 1584), which included a description of contemporary Ireland and an early history of Ireland to the time of Henry II, and *De Vita S. Patricii Hyberniae Apostoli,* a life of Saint Patrick (Antwerp, 1587). Although not much of a poet, Stanyhurst also turned his hand to verse. His hexameter translation of the first four books of Virgil's *Aeneid* (1582), based on his theory that quantity rather than accent should be the guiding principle of English meter, is still considered one of the most bizarre and ludicrous examples of Renaissance poetic experiment.

While in the Netherlands, Stanyhurst openly converted to Catholicism and became a pensioner of the Spanish crown. Sometime before 1585, he married Helen Copley, who belonged to one of the more important families of the English Catholic expatriate community in the Netherlands. His writings on Ireland and his growing reputation as a physician brought him to the attention of Philip II in 1590. He became an advisor on Irish affairs to the Spanish king and was involved in a number of conspiracies against Elizabeth's reign hatched within the English and Irish Catholic expatriate community and supported by the Spanish. After his second wife's death in 1602, he was ordained a Catholic priest and became one of the court chaplains to the archducal couple, Albert and Isabella, a position he held until his death in 1618.[12]

Stanyhurst's history became the first in a series of *Chronicles* contributions subject to official scrutiny. In December 1577, the Privy Council ordered John Aylmer, bishop of London, to summon the printer of a history of Ireland by "one Stanhurste" to discover how many of the histories had been printed, how many had been sold in Ireland, and how many remained unsold. The Privy Council claimed that in the history, "[M]any thinges are falcelie recited and contrarie to the ancient records of the said realm." Gerald Fitzgerald, Stanyhurst's employer, was ordered at the same time to send Stanyhurst to the Privy Council for questioning. In his appearance before the council, Stanyhurst offered to amend the offending passages, and the *Chronicles* were allowed to be distributed and sold after this was accomplished (*Irish,* xvi-xvii; Patterson 1994, 11–12).

John Stow

Because of the success of the 1577 *Chronicles,* its surviving publishers, John Harrison and George Bishop, decided to form a new syndicate and publish an expanded and revised edition. Since William Harrison was the only member left of the original group of contributors, the syndicate turned to some of the leading antiquarians of the day to continue the project. The most accomplished of these later contributors was John Stow, who had actually been involved, albeit indirectly, in the 1577 edition.

It is important to remember that in the absence of public libraries or collections, the manuscripts that these chroniclers and antiquarians used were most often purchased out of their own funds over an extended period. Wolfe himself had spent over two decades collecting manuscripts and maps for his chronology. John Stow, who purchased Wolfe's collection after the printer's death but lent parts of it as well as "divers rare monuments, ancient writers, and necessary register-books" from his own collection to Holinshed to use in the 1577 *Chronicles,* had impoverished himself in his lifelong pursuit of manuscripts, printed books, documents, charters, and antiquities. Stow contributed to the 1587 edition as a writer, continuing Holinshed's history of England to 1586. The time that he spent on the *Chronicles* appears to have slowed him in his own work, and at the end of his 1605 *Annals of England,* he expresses his resentment at having been anticipated in publishing an extended chronology of England when he refers to the printing and reprinting "without warrant or well liking" of Wolfe's materials under the name of "Raphael Holinshead his Chronicles."[13]

Of all the contributors to the project, Stow's origins were the humblest. The son of a tallow chandler, he was born about 1525 in the parish of St. Michael, Cornhill, London. He was trained as a tailor and was admitted to the Merchant Taylors' Company in 1547 but never was called to the livery or held any office. An autodidact, in his middle years he decided to devote himself "to the search of our famous antiquities." From 1560 to his death in 1605, Stow amassed a collection of printed books, legal and literary documents, charters, manuscripts, and inscriptions, all dealing with English history, archaeology, and literature.

His collection of medieval manuscripts brought him to the attention of Archbishop Parker, and Stow edited some of them for publication under the archbishop's direction. Included in these were Matthew of Westminster's *Flores Historiarum* (1567), Matthew Paris's *Chronicle* (1571), and Thomas Walsingham's *Chronicle* (1574), all of which were later used and cited by Holinshed in the 1577 edition of the *Chronicles.* Stow's editorial work for Parker brought him into association with Reyner Wolfe and the documents that he bought after Wolfe's death.

As Stow's patron, Parker introduced him to many of the leading antiquarians of his time, among them William Camden and William Lambarde, whose *Perambulation of Kent* was the model for Stow's *Survey of London* (Kingsford, 1908, xx). When the Society of Antiquaries was formed in the early 1570s under Archbishop Parker's patronage, Stow became a member. Among his colleagues in the society was Francis Thynne, another leading antiquarian and a contributor to Holinshed's *Chronicles.*

Stow's association with Parker no doubt helped him with his occasional brushes with the law. Stow, who if not a crypto-Catholic was most certainly a religious conservative, had a number of lawsuits brought against him, three of which appear to be religiously motivated. The earliest recorded one, which occurred before his acquaintance with Parker, was in 1544, during Henry VIII's reign, when a priest brought a false accusation, now unknown, against him. Stow was later able to have his accuser convicted of perjury in Star Chamber. In 1568 Stow was charged with being in possession of a copy of the Duke of Alva's manifesto against Elizabeth, which the Spanish ambassador had published and circulated in London. Stow was called before the lord mayor on 17 February 1568 or 1569. In the record of his examination, which describes him as "John Stowe, merchaunt, a collector of cronycles," he confessed that he had been lent two copies of the bill in English, had made a copy for himself, and had even read it to some neighbors, but had never actually circulated a copy. As a result, Stow was not punished. Later that month he was reported to the Queen's Council for having many dangerous books of superstition in his possession, and his house was ordered to be searched. On 24 February, Edmund Grindal, Bishop of London sent to

William Cecil, Lord Burghley, a "catalogue of Stowe the Taylour his unlawfulle bookes" and a report from his chaplains, dated 21 February, the day the search was made. Among Stow's library were listed "a great sorte of old written English Chronicles both in parchment and in paper," "Miscellanea of diverse sortes both touching phisicke, surgerye, and herbes, with medicines of experience, and also touching old phantasticall popish bokes prynted in the olde tyme, with many such also written in olde Englisshe on parchement," "such bokes as have been lately putt forth in the realme or beyonde the Seas for defence of papistrye: with a note of som of his own devises and writinges touching such matter as he hath gathered for Chronicles, whereabout he seemeth to have bestowed much travaile. His bokes declare him to be a great favourer of papistrye" (Kingsford 1908, xvi–xvii). Despite these discoveries, it does not appear that Cecil or the council thought the situation serious enough to require further investigation.

In 1570, Stow's brother Thomas, with whom he had always had an acrimonious relationship, and a former servant of Stow's gave information that led to yet another summons before the ecclesiastical commission, but the unspecified charge, which apparently again attacked Stow's religious orthodoxy, was satisfactorily disproved by Stow before the archbishop.

Although best known for his antiquarian pursuits and his *Survey of London* (1598), a detailed and invaluable record of Elizabethan London, John Stow was the most prolific chronicler of the sixteenth century. His career as a writer began in 1562 when he acquired a manuscript of the *Tree of Commonwealth* by Edmund Dudley, grandfather of Robert Dudley (later, the Earl of Leicester). He made his own copy and presented it to the author's grandson. Robert Dudley suggested that Stow pursue original historical writing, and Stow took his advice, beginning work on the chronicles that he would work on intermittently for the rest of his life. Besides his work on the 1587 edition of Holinshed's *Chronicles,* to which Stow contributed material for an update of English history from 1576 to 1586, he published 21 editions and issues of chronicles in three different formats, including an octavo of *A Summary of English Chronicles* (1565), a sextodecimo abridgment of the *Summary,* and in quarto, the *Annals of England* (1592). The text of his *Annals* is derived almost verbatim from his contributions to the *Chronicles,* which he cross-references to "my continuation of Master Reyne Woolfe, and Holinsheds chronicle."[14]

Stow's contributions to antiquarian studies brought him honor and recognition, not only among the learned but among his fellow citizens as well. The Merchant Taylors' Company awarded him a pension of 4 pounds annually in 1592. In 1600 the amount was raised to 10 pounds, and in 1602 it was renewed even though Stow was no longer working as a tailor, for "nowithstanding in his begynnyng was of the handy craft and now for many yeres hath spent great labour and study in writing of Chronicles and other memorable matters for the good of all posterity" (Kingsford 1908, xxiv-xxv). Nevertheless, for all his reknown, Stow ended his life in relative poverty.[15]

John Hooker

John Hooker (alias Vowell), a native of Exeter, although earlier believed to have been general editor of the *Chronicles,* appears to have contributed only to the expansion and update of the Irish history as well as those sections of the English history pertaining to the city of Exeter. Hooker came from a family of prominent landowners and officeholders in Exeter. Both his grandfather and his father had held the office of mayor, and his nephew was the theologian Richard Hooker. In the first half of his life, John used the last name "Vowell," which had come into the family from Pembroke as the result of a number of marriages to heiresses, and the alias Hooker. In his later life, he referred to himself as "John Hooker alias Vowell."

Born in 1524, he attended Oxford, where he studied law; traveled to the Continent, where he studied in Cologne; sojourned in Strasbourg with the Reformation theologian Peter Martyr; and later went to France. When he returned home, he devoted himself to the study of English history and astronomy, and in 1555 he was elected the first chamberlain of Exeter, an office that concerned the care of orphans, the safekeeping of records, the attending of city audits, and the surveying of city properties, among other duties. In 1568, he was retained as a solicitor by Sir Peter Carew, an English colonialist and military commander engaged in the suppression of Irish rebels, to recover some lands in Ireland that Carew claimed his medieval ancestors had long since lost. Because of the records that Hooker "discovered" in Waterford and Dublin, Carew was able to assume the title to the Barony of Idrone, settle on his reclaimed estate, and reward Hooker with land, patronage, and a seat in the Irish Parliament in 1568. After his term was completed, Hooker returned to his birthplace, where he spent the rest of his life. In April 1571, he was elected to represent Exeter in Parliament. He held several other local offices, including those of coroner and recorder, and retained the office of chamberlain in Essex until his death in 1601.[16]

Many of Hooker's contributions to the *Chronicles* are based on his personal experiences. In the English history, his contributions relate primarily to the region of Exeter, including a description of the Western Rebellion and his eyewitness account of the siege. The Western Rebellion, a popular uprising that occurred in response to Edward VI's and Somerset's religious reforms, began in the spring of 1549 in Cornwall, spread eastward into Devon, and ended with a march on Exeter and a siege of that city that began in the final days of June and lasted until mid-August. Hooker, then 24, participated in the defense of Exeter and soon afterward, at the city magistrates' request, wrote what is still considered the most complete and accurate account of the Western Rebellion. This account was later incorporated into the *Chronicles* (Snow 1977, 8–9). Hooker's other contributions to the English history included a description of the city of Exeter and a catalog of the bishops of Exeter.

Hooker's contributions to the Irish section of the *Chronicles* include the "Order and Usage of Keeping the Parliaments in England," a translation of Giraldus Cambrensis's *Expugnatio Hibernica* (Conquest of Ireland), and a continuation of the Irish history from 1546, where it had originally ended in the 1577 *Chronicles,* to 1586. As with his contributions to the English history, much of what he wrote for the update of the Irish history was inspired by his own experiences in that country. His chaotic tenure in the Irish House of Commons led him to write the "Order and Usage" and an account of his parliamentary experiences in his updating of the *Chronicles'* Irish history (Snow, 13–15). Hooker's election to the Irish Parliament in 1568, even though he was not a resident of Athenry, the borough he represented, was an example of one of the many irregular election practices that the Irish members of Parliament cited in their contention that the Irish House of Commons was an illegal assembly. Hooker evoked even more Irish hostility by speaking vehemently in favor of Poynings' Law, enacted under Henry VIII, which declared that no legislative action could be undertaken by the Irish Parliament unless it had already been approved by the English Crown. His long-winded defense of this law during a session in which the Irish members were pushing for its repeal so enraged the Opposition that Hooker was driven from Parliament, and, under the protection of his friends (including James Stanyhurst, then Speaker of the House), was forced to seek refuge in the house of his patron, Carew.[17]

Abraham Fleming

Hooker's exact role in the 1587 *Chronicles* is difficult to ascertain. Although he has traditionally been credited with the editorship of the 1587 version, there is no real evidence that he performed this service except that according to the title page of that edition, editorial credit is given to Hooker and "others." Recent scholarship has proven that Abraham Fleming served as editor, indexer, and "learned corrector." Fleming's contributions appear throughout the text, whereas Hooker's are limited to the expansion and update of the Irish history and some additions to the English history. Fleming's extensive experience in publishing as well as the nature of his contributions to the *Chronicles* support his position as editor of the later edition.

Fleming was born in London around 1552. He started his studies at Cambridge in 1570 but did not complete his bachelor's degree until 1581 or 1582, a delay probably caused by his steady employment in the London printing houses from 1575 to 1589. He began his career in printing in the service of Richard Tottel, but his tenure with Tottel seems to have been relatively short. His work appears in the publications of several printers, including all members of the syndicate that produced the second edition of Holinshed's *Chronicles*. In fact, Henry Denham, the printer of the 1587 *Chronicles*, produced a number of books between 1579 and 1589 that show Fleming acting in various capacities, suggesting that Fleming may have been in Denham's service during this time. Among the duties that Fleming carried out for various printing houses were those of poet, translator, editor, compiler, indexer, and, finally, "learned corrector," or proofreader (Donno 1989, 202).

Although not much of a poet, Fleming was an accomplished antiquarian and had 59 published texts to his credit, including original works, translations of Latin works into English, corrections and additions to the works of others, as well as indexes and addresses to the reader. A brief survey of his work, which includes such titles as "The Diamond of Devotion," "A Straunge and Terrible Wunder wroght very late in the Parish Church of Bongay," "Of all Blasing Starrs in Generall," and "Poetical translations for Reginald Scot's 'Discovery of Witchcraft,'" reveals a fascination with both religious matters and supernatural phenomena, both of which play a significant role in his additions to the *Chronicles*.[18] In 1588, Fleming decided to switch careers; he took religious orders and began service as chaplain to the Countess of Nottingham. In 1593 he became rector of St. Pancras, Soper Lane. He died in Leicestershire in 1607.

Fleming's work with Denham during the years of 1579 to 1589, along with his extensive editorial experience, would support the claim that he served as editor of the *Chronicles.* As William Miller has pointed out, Fleming's literary career appears to have ended at the same time that Denham's imprint disappears from the trade. Denham had three presses in 1586, but by 1589 he appears to have left the book trade. Coincidentally, Fleming's last published work appeared in 1589 (Miller, 90).

Another discovery that also appears to prove his editorial role involves two bound copies of proof sheets of Holinshed's *Chronicles,* which were acquired in 1987 by the Huntington Library in San Marino, California. Elizabeth Donno's examination of the printed text as well as these proof sheets reveals that Fleming's editorial duties included, in addition to compiling and organizing the texts, preparing the extensive indexes for the three volumes (apart from the contributions on Ireland by Hooker, who had indexed them himself) and carefully proofreading the texts and performing the necessary splicing and substitution of materials due to the censorship of the 1587 edition (Donno 1989, 201).

The practice in the *Chronicles* of indicating the original authorship of a section in the margin also reinforces Fleming's claims, since the vast majority of the insertions bear his initials. For example, as Donno has also pointed out, insertions taken from Grafton's *Abridgement,* Stow's *Summary,* and other sources bear such marginal notations as "Abr. Fl. ex I.F. [*Martyrologia*]" (Donno 1989, 205). Such marginal notations would seem to argue against Hooker or even Stow as editor, since specific materials attributed to these authors refer to them as a third party. For example, with regard to the civil uprisings of 1470, Fleming refers to "a verie good note or addition receiued from the hands of maister Iohn Hooker, chamberlaine of Excester" (*Chronicles* 3:676), and Hooker's account of the 1549 Devon uprising in the narrative of Edward VI's reign bears the following editorial note: "We adde a new report (new I meane, in respect of the publication, having not heretofore beene printed) though old enough, and sufficiently warranted by the reporter, who upon his owne notice hath delivered no lesse in writing" (3:936). As Patterson has pointed out, the use of the editorial "we" by Fleming and the reference to Hooker as "the reporter" who has "delivered" his account in writing again points to Fleming as editor (Patterson 1994, 9–10).

Francis Thynne

The final antiquarian to join the 1587 authors was Francis Thynne, whose primary contribution to the English history was a series of catalogs of various dignitaries and historical figures. Thynne also contributed to the Scottish history, updating it from 1571 to 1586 and adding new passages to the existing text taken from the *Rerum Scoticarum Historia,* published in 1582 by the Calvinist George Buchanan, and the *De Origine Moribus et Rebus Gestis Scotorum,* published in 1578 by the Catholic Archbishop of Ross, John Leslie.

Thynne, who sometimes referred to himself as Boteville, was the son of William Thynne, the famous editor of Chaucer. He was born about 1545 and studied at both Oxford and Cambridge. He was admitted as a member of Lincoln's Inn in 1561 and during his tenure there became close friends with Thomas Egerton, later Lord Ellesmere and lord chancellor. Although he became an attorney, it does not appear that he ever practiced law. His interests lay in poetry and literature, and later in the study of history and antiquities. Like Stow, he became a member of the Society of Antiquaries, which he joined in 1592. In 1602 he became Lancaster herald, a position he held probably because of his association with William Cecil, Lord Burghley.

Like other contributors to the *Chronicles,* Thynne had his brushes with the law, but this was due to financial troubles rather than any wrongdoing on his part. Toward the end of 1573, his books were dispersed and he was sent to prison for a debt of one hundred pounds. On 13 March and again on 19 March 1576, he wrote to Lord Burghley begging for help in his distress. In his letter, he claims that his kinsmen had withheld from him two hundred marks a year for four years under the pretext of providing for the assurance of his wife's jointure. Thynne was finally released from prison and attained a certain measure of respectability for the remainder of his life, as shown by his membership in the Society of Antiquaries and his heraldship. He died in 1608.[19]

Thynne has the dubious distinction of being the contributor whose work was most heavily excised by the censors of the 1587 edition. Four of the extensive catalogs that he had compiled were ordered deleted by the Privy Council. These included "The Lives of the Archbishops of Canterbury," "A Discourse of the Earles of Leicester," "A Treatise of the Lord Cobhams," and "The Catalog of the Lord Wardens of the Cinque Ports." His continuation of the Scottish history was censored as well.

Financing the *Chronicles*

It is important to remember that the *Chronicles'* existence was due not only to the efforts of its writers and compilers, but also to the financing of the entrepreneurs who backed it. The project itself had been initiated not by royal commission as had such works as Polydore Vergil's *Anglica Historia* or Edward Hall's *Union of the Two Noble and Illustre Famelies of Lancastre and Yorke,* but by commercial printers who would have expected a return on their investment. In fact, the existence of the 1587 edition is due directly to the financial success of the 1577 edition, which in turn owed its existence to Reyner Wolfe's financial success as a printer. Wolfe's personal wealth had enabled him to purchase the manuscripts, books, and maps that he needed to make such a project viable. In the absence of public libraries or collections, only individual purchasing power or aristocratic patronage would enable someone to have access to the materials necessary for such a text. As mentioned earlier, Wolfe purchased collections from the antiquarian John Leland for his *Universal Cosmography* after Leland's death, and in turn Stow purchased a good portion of Wolfe's collection for his own work after Wolfe's death. The importance of capital in the production of the *Chronicles* cannot be overemphasized. In a sense, that, more than the social status of its contributors, is what defines the text as a middle-class endeavor.

The financiers who supplied the capital for Holinshed's *Chronicles* were, for the most part, well-respected and well-known members of their profession. The three original backers, John Harrison, Lucas Harrison, and George Bishop, were all prosperous, prominent printers and booksellers, with close personal and business ties to Reyner Wolfe. John Harrison had married Wolfe's daughter Mary, and Lucas Harrison, John's half-brother, leased his shop from Wolfe.[20] Both Harrisons were executors of Wolfe's and his wife Joan's wills. Bishop, a business associate of Wolfe, was also an executor of his will as well as a witness to it.[21]

Although information concerning the Harrisons is scarce, we do know that Bishop was one of the most influential and prolific publishers of his day. In 1587, he was chosen by Christopher Barker as one of the deputies to manage the Queen's Printing House, and he rose to the highest positions in the Company of Stationers, serving as warden in 1577–1558 and 1583–1584 and master of the company for at least five times in 1589–1590, 1592–1593, 1599–1600, 1602–1603, and 1607–1608. He was also elected an alderman of the city of London. His most notable venture, besides Holinshed's *Chronicles,* was Hakluyt's *Voyages.*[22]

After Lucas Harrison's death, George Bishop and John Harrison decided to enlist three others to help finance the expanded and updated version of Holinshed's *Chronicles.* Thomas Woodcock, a bookseller, who along with Lucas and John Harrison was one of George Bishop's principal associates, had bought Lucas Harrison's rights to the 1577 *Chronicles* from Harrison's widow. Woodcock had further ties to the original syndicate. Like the Harrisons and Bishop, he had a close business association with Wolfe and was George Bishop's brother-in-law, both men having married daughters of John Cawood, the Queen's printer (McKerrow, 300, 335). Woodcock was imprisoned in 1578 for selling Cartwright's *Admonition to the Parliament* and was chosen as underwarden of the Stationer's Company in 1593 but died before his year of service expired (McKerrow, 300). Henry Denham, another of the new 1587 financial backers, also had problems with the law. Even though the products of his press were for the most part moralistic works and collections of private prayer, his own behavior appeared to be far from exemplary. He was fined in 1565 and 1584 for using indecorous language, and for improper behavior on other occasions. He was also fined in 1564 for printing unlicensed primers. Denham's lack of personal restraint did not exclude him from professional respectability, however. He was called to the livery of the Stationer's Company in 1572 and was appointed underwarden in 1586 and 1588.[23] Around 1574, he also acquired the patent from William Seres for printing the psalter, the primer for little children, and all books of private prayer in Latin and English (McKerrow, 89). The final financial backer added to the project was Ralph Newbery, a publisher and printer, who was in partnership with Henry Denham and Henry Bynneman, the printer of the first edition of the *Chronicles.* Newbery's name appeared on many of the most important publications of the day, including the *Chronicles,* Hakluyt's *Voyages,* and two editions of Stow's *Annals* (1592 and 1601).[24] Like Woodcock and Denham, he was an influential member of the Stationer's Company, serving as underwarden in 1583–1584 and again in 1584–1585 and as senior warden in 1589–1590 and 1590–1591. He became a master in 1598 and again in 1601 (McKerrow, 199).

Conclusion

As the lives of its various members demonstrate, the syndicate that gave us Holinshed's *Chronicles* was as multivoiced, extensive, and all-embracing as the opus it produced. Labeled a Protestant diatribe because of the contributions of Fleming and Harrison, at least two of the *Chronicles'* other major contributors, Stanyhurst and Stow, were known for their Roman Catholic sympathies. Dismissed as the work of the "excrement of the common people," the *Chronicles* counted parliamentarians, Anglo-Irish gentry, and clergy, as well as the leading antiquarians of its time, among its contributors.[25] In their marginal notes and comments, these writers and editors reveal the concerns of the gentry and citizen class as they strive to maintain their personal safety and equilibrium in a time of political and religious strife.

During the period of the *Chronicles'* compilation and publication, England was racked by a series of crises revolving around real or imagined conspiracies to remove Elizabeth I from the throne and to reestablish Catholicism in England. In the early years of her reign, Elizabeth followed a policy of religious compromise at home and managed to stay out of foreign entanglements with Catholic powers abroad. Yet her more extreme Catholic opponents both in England and on the Continent refused to recognize her legitimacy as Henry VIII's heir and England's sovereign. Her policy of accommodation came to an end in 1570 after the failure of the 1569 Northern Rebellion and with the issuance of Pope Pius V's bull *Regnans in excelsis,* which excommunicated Elizabeth, relieved her subjects of all loyalty to her, and advocated her violent overthrow. Ironically, the bull created a strong sense of national unity and Protestant determination as the English rallied around their beleaguered queen.

In 1571 anti-Catholic sentiment grew even greater when William Cecil, Elizabeth's most trusted secretary, exposed the Ridolfi plot, which sought to land six thousand Spaniards at Harwich to depose Elizabeth and crown Mary, Queen of Scots, queen of England. The arrival after 1574 of missionary priests recruited from among exiled English Catholics further fueled religious suspicion. The 1579 Desmond Rebellion, in which Irish forces led by the Catholic Earl of Desmond and an army of Italians and Spaniards financed by Pope Gregory XIII almost succeeded in driving the English out of Ireland, demonstrated how Pius V's bull could be appropriated by Irish rebels to oppose English rule. Furthermore, it confirmed England's fear that Continental Catholic powers could use Ireland to threaten national security and cut off western and southern sea routes.

The short period between 1583 and 1585 was especially marked by political turmoil. In 1583 the Privy Council ordered the torture of Francis Throckmorton, who implicated Mary, Queen of Scots; the Spanish ambassador Bernardino de Mendoza; and a number of Catholic nobles in a French plan to invade England. This conspiracy led Cecil, now Lord Burghley, and Francis Walsingham, secretary of state, to draft a bond of association in 1584. The association committed itself to defending Elizabeth and to pursuing and destroying all those who made any attempt on her life. Furthermore, it advocated the death of any successor who would benefit from an attempted assassination. Although the association was no more than a political vigilante group, thousands of members of the nobility and the gentry joined it. The existence of the association does not appear to have completely discouraged assassination conspiracies, for in 1585 William Parry, MP for Queenborough, stood trial for yet another plot to murder Elizabeth.

Despite the number of attempts on her life and throne, Elizabeth managed to resist demands from her Protestant advisors to execute Mary, Queen of Scots, for Elizabeth did not want to be implicated in the death of a fellow monarch. Her hand was finally forced by the Babington conspiracy of 1586. Revealed by Walsingham, the conspiracy implicated Mary with a letter in which she supposedly endorsed Elizabeth's assassination. The other conspirators were quickly tried and hanged, but while Mary was convicted of treason in October 1586, Elizabeth postponed her kinswoman's execution until February 1587, when rumors that the Spanish had landed in Wales and that Mary had escaped from prison finally compelled her to sign the death warrant.

The events of the 1570s and 1580s prompted some of Elizabeth's most trusted counselors, including Walsingham and Robert Dudley, Earl of Leicester, to advise Elizabeth to take a more militantly Protestant stand and a more active military role against the Continental Catholic powers. Despite their urging, Elizabeth managed to stay out of war until 1588, when Spain attempted to invade England with its Great Armada. The defeat of the armada and the execution of Mary finally ended any serious Catholic threat to Elizabeth's rule, but the years leading up to Elizabeth's final consolidation of power were fraught with anxiety and suspicion. The time during which Holinshed's *Chronicles* was written, published, expanded, and republished corresponds with this period of religious and political tension, and therefore the choice, interpretation, and placement of materials in both the 1577 and 1587 editions cannot be dismissed simply as the haphazard agglomeration of diverse sources but must be viewed as manifestations of conflicting religious, political, and national loyalties.

Chapter Two

The "Historie of England"

Tudor historians tended to evaluate the past in terms of its lessons for the present. Edward Hall's *Union of the Two Noble and Illustre Famelies of Lancastre and Yorke,* which related the history of the War of the Roses, was a warning to those who wished to avoid civil chaos and preserve political stability, while Bale's and Foxe's histories of the English church proved the purity of the English ecclesiastical tradition as well as Rome's ancient and continuing threat to its existence. At the same time, the Tudor dynasty sponsored its own myths of ancient origin through the officially patronized writings of Hall and Polydore Vergil's *Anglica Historia* to validate its somewhat shaky claim to the throne. While Tudor Histories such as these were written to promote specific agendas, Holinshed's *Chronicles'* "Historie of England" was written with a different purpose in mind. As Annabel Patterson has pointed out, the authors of the *Chronicles* strove to provide their readers with the means to interpret and evaluate the past for themselves by including as much documentary evidence as possible, thus enabling their readers to draw their own lessons from history (Patterson 1994, 7–8). This is not to say that these authors refrained from suggesting or overtly stating their own points of view, for they often did so. Nevertheless, they incorporated numerous and occasionally differing perspectives into their text, whether they agreed with them or not.

To accomplish their goal, the authors had to collect as many sources as possible and present them within the history. As evidenced by the 180 references listed in the introductory pages of the narrative, the authors of Holinshed's "Historie of England" strove to create the most comprehensive historical chronicle of its time. The English history not only draws on existing classical, medieval, and contemporary histories, but it also includes "Records and rolles diverse" as well as such ephemera as pamphlets, proclamations, and official edicts. The authors incorporated primary texts whenever possible, including numerous eyewitness accounts. They often included two or three sources, even if they conflicted, for the same event. Some sources were paraphrased, others copied almost verbatim. Some sections of the history were formed from the composite work of a number of source authors; others, such as the history of the later Plantagenets and the early Tudors, drew primarily on one source, in this case, Edward Hall's *Union.* Despite the fact that they worked with such a large number of texts, the authors were very careful to document their work. In addition to the list at the beginning of the history, they included extensive marginal notes indicating their sources.

The "Historie of England" is certainly the best-known portion of Holinshed's *Chronicles,* primarily because of its role as a resource for Shakespeare and other English authors. The history is divided into two parts: the creation of the world through the Norman Conquest, and the reign of William the Conqueror through the reign of Elizabeth I. In length, the "Historie of England" forms the greatest part of the *Chronicles,* comprising two-thirds of both editions. Approximately half of the 1587 English history is devoted to the Tudor century from 1485 to 1587. Obviously, the history's emphasis is on current events, specifically those historical occurrences that shaped the world in which the contributors and their audience lived. Although the "Historie of England" notably emphasized contemporary affairs over earlier events, it still provided a sense of historical perspective and made England's medieval past available to a wider audience than ever before.

The 1577 "Historie of England"

Raphael Holinshed dedicated his 1577 "Historie of England" to William Cecil, Lord Burghley, then lord treasurer and member of the Privy Council. In his dedication, Holinshed states his historical methodology, which is to provide the reader with as comprehensive a text as possible. He admits that he "was loth to omit anie thing that might increase the readers knowledge" and excuses himself for not having "so orderlie disposed" his materials as "otherwise I ought; choosing rather to want order, than to defraud the reader of that which for his further understanding might seeme to satisfie his expectation."

Despite the occasionally haphazard ordering of his materials, Holinshed's history is characterized by the clarity and directness of its narrative. Holinshed often eschews the descriptive or discursive elements of his sources and instead focuses on the action. He lets the text speak for itself, refraining, for the most part, from judgmental evaluation. He is a master of objectivity and understatement, and as he mentions in his "Preface to the Reader," his mission is to present his readers with all available information so that they may draw their own conclusions: "First concerning the historie of England, as I have collected the same out of manie and sundrie authors, in whome what contrarietie, negligence, and rashnesse sometime is found in their reports; I leave to the discretion of those that have perused their works: for my part, I have in things doubtfull rather chosen to shew the diversitie of their writings, than by over-ruling them, and using a peremptorie censure, to frame them to agree to my liking: leaving it neverthelesse to each mans judgement, to controll them as he seeth cause." At the same time, Holinshed clearly notes which of his sources can be trusted and which cannot, thus leading readers toward or away from a particular interpretation of history or at least suggesting that they evaluate certain information with some skepticism. Holinshed was not a credulous and indiscriminating gatherer of material, nor does he leave his readers entirely to their own judgment.

This quality is particularly apparent in Holinshed's depiction of England's earliest inhabitants. Drawn primarily from the work of John Bale and Geoffrey of Monmouth, the first section of the English history includes such fantastical figures as Samothes, Noah's grandson and the first human to arrive in England; the giant Albion, after whom England was originally named; Aeneas's grandson Brute, who with his Trojans conquered Albion's race of giants and created the kingdom of Britain; and Brennius and Belinus, who, according to Geoffrey of Monmouth, invaded imperial Rome. Holinshed often articulates his discomfort with these tales, opening his history with the warning that "sith the originall in maner of all nations is doubtfull, and even the same for the more part fabulous (that alwaies excepted which we find in the holie scriptures) I wish not any man to leane to that which shall be here set downe as to an infallible truth, sith I doo but onlie shew other mens conjectures, grounded neverthelesse upon likelie reasons, concerning that matter whereof there is now left but little other certeintie, or rather none at all" (*Chronicles,* 1:427). Later he notes of these fabulous accounts, "I leave it to the consideration of the reader, to thinke thereof as reason shall move him sith I see not how either in this, or in other things of such antiquitie, we cannot have sufficient warrant otherwise than by likelie conjectures" (1:436). Although he diligently includes all the myths and legends of ancient Britain in his history, Holinshed implies that the intelligent reader will dismiss most of these stories as false. One can almost hear his sigh of relief when he turns to the Roman invasion under Julius Caesar and states, "[N]ow are we come to the time in the which what actes were atchived, there remaineth more certeine record, and therefore may we the more boldlie proceed in this our historie" (1:464).

Despite his access to "more certeine record," Holinshed continues to express suspicions about his sources' veracity well beyond the section dealing with the Roman occupation. He dismisses King Arthur, "of whom the trifling tales of the Britains even to this day fantasicallie doo descant and report woonders," although in pointing out those few elements of the legend that appear to be true, he admits, "[W]oorthie was he doubtlesse, of whom feined fables should not have so dreamed, but rather that true histories might have set foorth his woorthie praises, as he that did for a long season susteine and hold up his countrie that was readie to go to utter ruine and decaie" (*Chronicles,* 1:579). Holinshed's inclusion of this material does not mean that he believed it to be true, and his numerous comments on its dubious veracity reveal his critical stance. He appears to have regarded the histories of the early kings as cultural knowledge and perhaps moral instruction, but not factual information. In citing various and often contradictory authorities and including such obviously false and ridiculous material, Holinshed provided his readers with an understanding of England's cultural legacy. Whether true or false, these stories ultimately defined the society in which his audience lived and the way in which it viewed the world.

Although Holinshed clearly doubts the historical truth concerning many of ancient England's monarchs, he draws examples from their reigns to illustrate a number of moral and political lessons. Of primary concern was the social and political chaos caused by civil discord and the importance of avoiding internecine war. From the legendary period of the first kings of Britain through the final days of the Plantagenets, a pattern appears in which familial struggles over the throne lead to wider dissension and the ultimate ruin of the country. Leir's grandsons Cunedag and Margan capture and imprison their aunt Cordelia in order to seize the monarchy from her and then fall to quarreling themselves (*Chronicles,* 1:448). On the eve of the Danish invasions, the Mercian king Offa kills his new son-in-law, Ethelbert of the Eastangles (1:649). Princess Quendred has her seven-year-old brother, Kenelm, assassinated because of her jealousy over his accession to the crown of Mercia (1:659). Queen Alfred murders her stepson, King Edward of England, so that her own son, Egelred, might reign (1:699). Even under the Norman and Plantagenet kings this pattern continues. Henry II's later years are characterized by civil discord as his sons band together in rebellion against him. The Plantagenet dynasty self-destructs as the Houses of Lancaster and York battle for supremacy.

Holinshed also depicts how England's internal dissension not only weakened it from within but left it vulnerable to foreign attack. The country's early history is characterized by waves of succeeding invaders. The pattern of invasion, conquest, and decay applies to Britons, Romans, Saxons, Danes, and Normans. Holinshed demonstrates how as each kingdom became corrupted, civil dissension broke out, weakening it from within. Unable to withstand foreign attack, the beleaguered nation was vanquished by a new, stronger, and often morally superior invader who then established a new regime. In turn, that kingdom became weak, corrupt and marred by civil turmoil and with the passing of time was in turn invaded itself. Holinshed compares this pattern to the growth and decline of an aging body in his narrative of the Normans' invasion of England during the rule of Ethelred the Unready:

> This Egelred or Etheldred was the 30 in number from Cerdicus the first king of the Westsaxons: through his negligent government, the state of the commonwealth fell into such decaie . . . that under him it may be saide, how the kingdome was come to the uttermost point or period of old and feeble age . . . For wheras, whilest the realme was divided at the first by the Saxons into sundrie dominions, it grew at length (as it were increasing from youthfull yeeres) to one absolute monarchie, which passed under the late remembred princes, Egbert, Adelstane, Edgar, and others, so that in their daies it might be said, how it was growne to mans state, but now under this Egelred, through famine, pestilence, and warres, the state thereof was so shaken, turned upside downe, and weakened on ech part, that rightlie might the season be likened unto the old broken yeeres of mans life, which through feeblenesse is not able to helpe it selfe. (*Chronicles*, 1:703)

Holinshed continuously depicts England's cycle of invasions as the result of internal dissension and corruption. In his "Preface to the Reader," he notes that the Romans easily conquered Britain "by reason of the factions amongst the princes of the land, which the Romans (through their accustomed skill) could turne verie well to their most advantage." The Saxon invasion of Britain occurred because of "the wicked sins and unthankefulnesse of the inhabitants towards God, the cheefe occasions and causes of the transmutations of kingdoms." The Danes were able to invade because the Saxons "fell at division among themselves, and often-times with warre pursued ech other, so as no perfect order of governement could be framed." Finally, the Normans succeeded due to the fact that "by the insolent dealings of the governours, a division was made betwixt the king and his people, through just punishment decreed by

the providence of the Almightie, determining for their sinnes and contempt of his lawes, to deliver them into the hands of a stranger; and
therueupon when spite and envie had brought the title in doubt, to
whom the right in succession apperteined, the Conqueror entred." The
threat of foreign invasion does not disappear with the establishment of
the Norman kingdom, for as Holinshed reveals, the civil discord of
John I's reign opened the door to French and papal interference.

In the "Historie of England," civil turmoil is the worst evil that can
befall the land, and the examples Holinshed draws from the reigns of
English monarchs illustrate this lesson repeatedly. Family violence is not
the only source of civil strife. As the history proceeds, Holinshed clearly
demonstrates that both the monarch and his people have a mutual
responsibility to preserve peace and accord through the keeping of their
respective obligations. The failure of one party or the other to do so results
in political chaos. Even when depicting the reigns of such completely disastrous monarchs as Ethelred II, Holinshed notes that both king and subject are responsible for the country's problems: "But what is a king if his
subjects be not loiall? What is a realme, if the common wealth be divided?
By peace & concord, of small beginnings great and famous kingdomes
have oft times proceeded; whereas by discord the greatest kingdoms have
oftner bene brought to ruine" (*Chronicles,* 1:708). This lesson becomes one
of the major themes of the narrative concerning John I's reign. Holinshed's account preserves the traditional sixteenth-century presentation of
John as a kind of proto-Reformer and precursor to Henry VIII in his
struggles with Rome, but there is a distinct emphasis on the mutual
responsibility of John and his subjects for his calamitous reign. Holinshed
notes how John was "bountifull and liberall unto strangers, but of his
owne people (for their dailie treasons practised towards him) a great
oppressour, so that he trusted more to forreners than to them, and therfore in the end he was of them utterlie forsaken" (2:339).

The reigns of Edward II and Richard II also depict the dangers of
civil unrest, and as in his narrative of John I's reign, Holinshed faults the
barons and the commoners as much as the king for the disasters that
ensue from a disunited realm. Both Edward and Richard are portrayed
negatively, but their vices are blamed on the influence of evil counselors
and youthful folly. While Holinshed presents the barons' complaints
against the two monarchs sympathetically, at the same time he notes
that when "the barons and great lords agreed not in manie points
among themselves, and so being not of one mind . . . some danger
might grow to the state of the whole realme" (*Chronicles,* 2:773).

Holinshed's narrative repeatedly reveals a firm belief that ruler and ruled were bound in a symbiotic relationship of mutual obligations; the failure of the ruler as well as his subjects to honor this bond was one of the primary sources of civil strife. Holinshed seems particularly interested in those elements of feudalism that impacted the development of English constitutionalism, specifically the contractual rights and obligations between lord and vassal. He often criticizes kings who abused their power, particularly those who encroached on their subjects' rights. Holinshed does not present this lesson only by negative example, however. An anecdote that he offers concerning Edward I proves that such conflicts could be resolved peaceably.

Holinshed relates how in attempting to implement a scheme designed to raise money, Edward I declared that all who held land and tenements from him had to demonstrate by what title they held their properties. If they could not do so, the king planned to confiscate the lands to be sold or redeemed again. Edward did this knowing full well that over the course of time and because of the many civil wars that had racked England, many charters, deeds, copies, and other written documents had been lost, destroyed, or stolen. As the narrative notes, "Men in everie place made complaint and shewed themselves greevouslie offended, so that the king by meanes thereof came in great hatred of his people," yet since they had no evidence of title, no one dared complain. Only one man had the courage to remind the king of his feudal obligations:

> At length the lord John Warren earle of Surrie, a man greatlie beloved of the people, perceiving the king to have cast his net for a preie, and that there was not one which spake against him, determined to stand against those so bitter and cruell proceedings. And therefore being called afore the justices about this matter, he appeared, and being asked, "by what right he held his lands?" suddenlie drawing foorth an old rustie sword; "By this instrument (said he) doo I hold my lands, and by the same I intend to defend them. Our ancestors comming into this realme with William the Conquerour, conquered their lands with the sword, and with the same will I defend me from all those that should be about to take them from me; he did not make a conquest of this realme alone, our progenitors were with him as participants and helpers."
>
> The king understanding into what hatred of his people by this meanes he was fallen, and therfore desirous to avoid civill dissention and war that might thereby insue, he left off his begun practise: so that the thing which generallie should have touched and beene hurtfull to all men, was

now suddenlie staied by the manhood and couragious stoutnesse onelie
of one man. (*Chronicles,* 2:483–84)

The preceding anecdote never states, but certainly suggests, that the
king's authority was not absolute but was held from the people, and
that the land in dispute was not merely land but a symbol of the pledge
between monarch and subject. Edward, in his attempt to seize his vas-
sals' land, risked losing his authority through the destruction of that
pledge. In feudalism, public rights and duties were tied to the tenure of
the land, and Edward clearly transgressed the limitations of his power in
unilaterally seizing land held in vassalage without justifiable cause, as
the Earl of Surrey asserted in his impassioned response. In transgressing
the limit, the king nullified the feudal tie and therefore released his subjects of any obligation to him. Although the earl was within his rights to
rebel, he first chose to remind the king of his obligations before doing
so, and Edward, to his credit, recognized the importance of his subjects'
happiness to his own political security. Placing the good of the commonwealth above his own personal interests and aware of the "civill dis-
sention and war that might thereby insue" if he continued seizing land,
he ceased his practice. Unlike the numerous other examples of conflict
between king and subject that appear in the "Historie of England," the
anecdote provides a paradigm for the proper relationship between ruler
and ruled.

Throughout the "Historie of England," Holinshed manages to present an impartial and unprejudiced narration of events, and in presenting conflicting opinions, he often includes both sides, even if it puts him
in the position of devil's advocate. In the case of Richard II, Holinshed
provides an objective recital of all of Richard's vices, noting that he was
"prodigall, ambitious, and much given to the pleasure of the bodie" and
that the extravagant living that characterized his court spread to "the
townes and Countreys . . . to the greate hynderaunce and decay of the
commonwealth." He also points to the corruption of the clergy during
his reign and how "there reigned abundantly the filthie sinne of lecherie
and fornication, with abominable adulterie, specially in the king, but
most chieflie in the prelacie." He presents Henry Bolingbroke's complaints against the king sympathetically, and his depiction of Henry and
the other barons' rebellion, Parliament's role in the deposition of
Richard, and Richard's handing over of the crown to Bolingbroke objectively and factually. He concludes his narrative with his own view of
Richard's reign: "Thus have ye heard what wryters do report touching

the state of the time and the doings of this king. But if I may boldly say what I think: he was a Prince the most unthankfully used of his subjects, of any one of whome ye shall lightly read." Holinshed goes on to point out that through youthful frailty and bad counselors Richard "demeaned himself more dissolutely than seemed convenient for his royall estate," but "yet in no kings days were the commons in greater wealth," nor "were the Nobles and Gentlemen more cherished nor the Churchmen lesse wronged." After noting the lack of gratitude and appreciation in Richard's subjects, Holinshed then criticizes Bolingbroke for being "chiefe instrument of this mischief" and for his "ambicious cruelty" in taking from Richard "his guiltlesse life" (*Chronicles*, 2:969). Holinshed's seeming sympathy for Richard at this point seems confusing. Does it point to a providential view of history since Holinshed mentions later that Bolingbroke and his line were punished later for their rebellion, or was it merely a prudent move on Holinshed's part to avoid the censors?[1] It could be argued that Holinshed's concern is not necessarily with the deposition of Richard itself but with the manner in which it was carried out and the refusal of both king and subjects to place the good of the commonwealth over personal interests. In fact, one of Holinshed's critiques of the open rebellion against Richard II is that the nobles "by strong hand, than by gentle and courteous meanes" attempted to control the king, "which stirred such malice betwixt him and them, till at length it could not be asswaged without perill of destruction to them both" (2:969). Holinshed's articulation of a perspective at odds with the traditional understanding of Richard II would enable readers to see both sides of the issue. Whatever the point of view, Holinshed's emphasis on the mutual destruction and ruin brought about by internal strife and his insistence on the importance of avoiding civil dissension create a cyclic pattern in the "Historie of England," reminding the reader that those who do not learn from the past are destined to repeat it. Although Holinshed usually refrains from overt commentary in his depiction of events, his arrangement of his narrative clearly presents this lesson to the reader.

The cyclic nature of Holinshed's history is more sophisticated than that of his medieval predecessors in that the repetition of events is obviously designed to do more than teach moral values or to demonstrate the workings of Providence in this world. The 1577 "Historie of England" is not particularly providential in its outlook, although Fleming's 1587 revisions later give the history a markedly providential tone in certain sections. The cycles of Holinshed's history teach a political lesson in that they demonstrate which behaviors should be avoided and which embraced to insure England's well-being. Holinshed focuses on the causes of civil dissension, its effects on the commonwealth, and the importance to a country's stability of avoiding dissension whenever possible. Human causation plays an important role in Holinshed's earlier text, and the morals that he draws from events, such as the reigns of Edward I, or even John I and Richard II, fully implicate human behavior in the workings of history. John's and Richard's falls are clearly caused by their own lack of good leadership as well as their subjects' intransigence. Although bad kings may deserve their fates, Holinshed suggests that the civil unrest that ensues is sometimes worse than poor leadership and that the health of the commonwealth is the primary responsibility of both the prince and the people.[2]

The appearance of omens, portents, and other supernatural wonders plays a role in the 1577 "Historie of England," though a less significant one than in the 1587 text. These phenomena are usually associated with national disasters, although they occasionally herald joyous occasions as well. Such portents and wonders foreshadow foreign attacks, as in the case of the Danish invasion where "there fell upon mens garments, as they walked abroad, crosses of bloudie colour, and bloud fell from heaven as drops of raine" (*Chronicles*, 1:653). They also accompany famines, regicides, wars, and civil unrest. The growing animosity that finally erupts into civil war between the Norman king William Rufus and his brother Robert is heralded by "manie grisely and uncouth sights . . . as hostes of men fighting in the skie with fierie beames flashing out, stars falling from heaven, and such other wonders" (Holin. 1577, 2:325r.). The reign of Stephen of Boulogne, noteworthy for its 17 years of civil war, also brings forth omens of chaos: "The same day in the which he arived in Englande, there chanced a mightie great tempest of thunder, with lightning marvelous, horrible to heare and to behold. And bycause this happened in the winter time, it seemed agaynst nature, and therefore it was the more noted as a foreshadowing of some trouble and calamity to come" (2:3656r). The linking of blazing stars, earthquakes, and other disturbances of nature with political disasters in the 1577 "Historie of England" creates a narrative pattern that highlights the repetitive nature of England's history.

Such natural wonders appeared in most of Holinshed's sources as manifestations of divine interference in human affairs, but Holinshed's portents serve more as narrative links highlighting the similarities between historical events than as manifestations of historical causation.

Omens and portents typically demonstrated how God foreshadowed human events with natural wonders, often as a warning of dangers to come. Unlike many historians of his time, including Fleming, who later glossed many of Holinshed's omens and portents to give them a moral significance, Holinshed rarely draws an overt connection between these phenomena and the events that they precede. When Holinshed supplies a moral explanation for a wonder preceding an historic event, he usually accompanies it with such qualifying phrases as "it seems" or "as hath been reported" rather than claiming such an explanation himself. In the 1577 "Historie of England" the emphasis is on the similarities of the wonders accompanying related historical events rather than on any particular moral significance they may have.

Holinshed's presentation of English history as cyclical is also developed by the formulaic nature of the numerous illustrations that adorn the pages of the 1577 "Historie of England." All three of the 1577 histories are distinguished by the inclusion of elaborate and detailed woodcuts used over and over again, often anachronistically, to portray significant events. Occasionally the wood prints, such as the one depicting Boadica addressing her troops before their last rebellion against the Romans, refer to a specific historical moment. The vast majority are vague enough in reference to illustrate a variety of different occasions, although they tend to focus on calamities or on displays of power, whether in acts of violence or courtly rituals. In the first part of the English history, small woodcut depictions of Britain's kings serve as chapter divisions, marking the reigns of succeeding monarchs. The illustrations are obviously not based on any realistic concept of portraiture, since the same pictures are continually repeated for different monarchs and can also be found in the Scottish history. The woodcuts' removal from the 1587 edition exemplifies the later editor's decision to redesign the "Historie of England" as a teleological rather than cyclical narrative, culminating in Elizabeth's triumphant reign.[3]

England's political history is the primary focus of the 1577 "Historie of England," but its ecclesiastical history is touched on as well. Holinshed does not give religious issues the importance that they receive in the 1587 version, but he does frame his history within a Protestant perspective. His church history focuses on those events proving the ancient establishment of a native religious tradition, such as Joseph of Arimathea's arrival in England to preach the gospel and baptize the native population, the struggles between the native British church and Augustine of Canterbury, the evangelizer of the Anglo-Saxons, Pope Honorius's decree permitting the archbishops of York and Canterbury to choose each others' successors without consulting Rome, and Bede's translation of the gospel of Saint John into English. Other incidents, such as Henry II's quarrel with Thomas à Becket and John I's, Henry III's, and Henry VIII's struggles with the papacy, appear, but they are treated factually and with restraint.

While the 1577 "Historie of England" lacks the religious histrionics that are one of the defining features of the 1587 edition, Holinshed includes his share of attacks on the Catholic clergy, but they are of a far more subtle nature. Holinshed seems particularly interested in examples of clerical corruption, and his choice and placement of material reveal this concern. When gathering material for his early English history, Holinshed drew his information from medieval sources, most of which were monastic and all of which were written from a Catholic perspective. Had Holinshed been a Reformist historian along the lines of John Bale, John Foxe, or even his own successor, Abraham Fleming, he would have either co-opted these sources, turning their evidence against itself to present an anti-Catholic bias and a revisionist view of church history, or he would have reframed the information in a scathing rhetorical display of antipapist sentiment, but this was not his method. This is not to say that Holinshed refrains from all religious commentary. In a manner similar to that in his asides cautioning his readers to consider the veracity of the sources he presents to them, Holinshed unobtrusively directs his audience toward a Protestant view of ecclesiastical history, primarily through his depiction of clerical vices.

Holinshed tends to criticize through marginal asides or anecdote rather than through the overt and distracting commentary that Fleming later employed, much to the 1587 narrative's disadvantage. In a story concerning Dunstan, abbot of Glastonbury, Holinshed incorporates the original medieval account into the main body of his text without remark on the supposed miracle that occurred. When the dying Anglo-Saxon king Edred issued a proclamation that all who had any of his treasure in keeping return it to him immediately so that he could dispose of it as he saw appropriate, Dunstan gathered what treasure he had and hurried to deliver it to the king, "but as he was upon the waie, a voice spake to him from heaven, saieng; Behold king Edred is now departed in peace. At the hearing of this voice, the horsse whereon Dunstane rode felle downe and died, being not able to abide the presence of the angell that thus spake to Dunstane. And when he came to the court, he understood that the king died the same houre in which it was told him by the angell"

(*Chronicles,* 1:692). In the margin, Holinshed cynically notes, "But was not this a devise thereby to deteine the treasure? for I doo not read that he delivered it out of his hands." Although the main text includes nothing derogatory in its account of Dunstan, Holinshed's marginalia clearly implies that the abbot's alleged miracle was an excuse to cover his greed.

In an anecdote from the reign of Henry III, Holinshed includes a trenchant critique of clerical corruption and a denial of the Pope's supremacy without adding one comment of his own. He relates how a Carthusian monk, "of honest conversation and sober," refused to attend divine service and was consequently imprisoned. When examined by a papal legate as to the reasons for his refusal, the monk "openlie protested, that Gregorie was not the true pope, nor head of the church, but that there was another head of the church, and that the church was defiled, so that no service ought to be said therein, except the same were newlie dedicated, and the vessels and vestments againe hallowed and consecreated; the divell (said he) is lose, & the pope is an heretike, for Gregorie, which nameth himselfe pope hath polluted the church." In response the legate asked him, "Is not power granted to our sovereigne lord the pope from above, both to lose and bind soules, sith he executeth the roome of S. Peter upon earth." The narrative succinctly presents the tense expectation surrounding the monk's reply as it describes how "all men looked to heare what answer he would make, beleeving his jugement to depend upon the same." The monk posed the counter-question, "How can I beleeve, that unto a person spotted with simonie and usurie, and haplie wrapt in more greevous sins, such power should be granted as was granted unto holie Peter, who immediatlie followed the lord, as soone as he was made his apostle, and followed him not onelie in bodilie footsteps, but in cleerenesse of vertues." In response, "the legat blushed, & said to some of the standers by; 'A man ought not to chide with a foole, nor gape over an oven' " (*Chronicles,* 2:389). While the papal legate and "diverse other worshipfull personages" dismissed the monk as an imbecile, the story makes very clear who the true fools are in not recognizing that the monk is referring to Christ as the other "head of the church." Furthermore, the narrative suggests that the legate's blush of shame, his inability to respond to the monk's query, and his choice not to condemn the monk for heresy but to dismiss him as a fool reveal that at some level, he realizes the truth of his adversary's utterances. Through the careful choice and inclusion of such anticlerical anecdotes, Holinshed presents England's religious history through a Protestant perspective while maintaining the objective tone that is the hallmark of his narrative.

Holinshed is far more reticent in his portrait of the Tudor period than he is in his depiction of ancient and medieval history. He draws no obvious lessons from the reigns of England's Renaissance monarchs and minimizes to an even greater degree the occasional moral commentary that occurs in the earlier portion of the history. Simple prudence would dictate such caution in approaching recent history, but even Mary Tudor, so often demonized in contemporary histories of the period, is treated with restraint and objectivity. Conversely, Elizabeth's reign, which the 1587 edition heralds as the triumphant manifestation of God's divine favor (although events included in the text would seem to indicate otherwise), appears simply as another step in the march of history.

The *Chronicles'* treatment of Henry VIII's tumultuous regime is a particularly cogent example of how Holinshed, even while avoiding political commentary or criticism, creates a sense of the tensions or dangers that characterized a particular ruler's reign. Based on Hall's text, the narrative of Henry VIII's reign is represented by three distinct stages. The first, which records the first 18 years of his government, depicts Henry as gracious and courtly, skilled in arms and games, well educated, a lover of courtly pastimes and entertainments, and a favorite of his people; Henry is the ideal Renaissance prince. This changes dramatically in the 18th year of his reign (1527), when the first questions are raised as to the legitimacy of his marriage to Catherine of Aragon. Henry is portrayed as concerned over the possibility that he has sinned and haunted by the fear that his lack of a male heir may be due to this sin. He finally, and very reluctantly, agrees to a divorce after consulting various experts about the legitimacy of his marriage. Anne Boleyn is not mentioned until after he has decided to divorce and therefore is not portrayed as one of the causes of the divorce. The last years of his reign, after the death of Catherine and the execution of Anne Boleyn, are characterized by numerous executions for heresy and treason. Although the text remains curiously silent on the details of these executions or the charges brought against the accused (information supplied in the accounts of all other reigns), the reader is struck by their number and frequency. In fact, the executions of the later years of Henry's reign offer a bleak counterpoint to the celebrations of the early years. The excessive violence of Henry's later rule is never commented on, only recited. When the narrative presents the traditional summary of the monarch's life and government at Henry's death, little is said, and instead of providing his own conclusion, Holinshed supplies John Leland's praise of Henry's largesse, all in Latin. The closing commentary on Henry's reign is notably shorter than that of his son, Edward, who ruled less than six years. Henry may be portrayed as the great religious reformer and Protestant champion in the *Chronicles,* but nonetheless, the most striking elements of his last years are the unrest, the rebellions, the executions, and the bloodshed. While the history may praise Henry as a "tresnoble and trespuissant" monarch, its narrative provides a less than ideal portrait of the king.

Holinshed relies on eyewitness accounts and anecdotes to supply color and interest to his Tudor narratives, and as Henry VIII's reign demonstrates, these become the reader's cue as to how a particular monarch should be evaluated. Holinshed's treatment of Mary Tudor's reign is notable for its impartiality, yet even here, in his typically under-stated way, he directs his readers' interpretation of events. In describing the general pardon that was proclaimed at the time of Mary's corona-tion, he notes that it was "interlaced with so manie exceptions as they that needed the same most, tooke smallest benefit thereby," thus point-ing out the emptiness of the gesture while hinting at Mary's subsequent persecution of her many enemies (*Chronicles,* 4:7). Holinshed's efforts to maintain an impartial presentation of his material can best be appreci-ated through comparing his portrayal of events to Fleming's report of the same. When relating the story of Mary Tudor's hysterical pregnancy, Holinshed makes no comments of his own as to the controversies sur-rounding the event nor does he draw any conclusions himself, but he includes the various conclusions drawn by others:

> And the sayde rumor continued so long that at the last, reporte was made, that shee was delyvered of a Prince and for joye thereof, Belles were roong, and Bonfires made, not only in the Citie of London, but also in sundrie places of the Realme, but in the ende, all proved cleane con-trarie, and the joy and expectation of the people utterly frustrate: for shortly it was fully certified (almost to all men) that the Queene was as then neyther delivered of a childe, nor after was in hope to have any.
>
> Of this people spake diversly.
>
> Some sayde, that the rumor of the Queenes conception was spread for a policie.
>
> Some affirmed that she was with childe, but it miscarried.
>
> Some other sayd that shee was deceived by a Timpany, or other lyke dis-ease; whereby shee thought shee was with childe, and was not. But what the troth was, I referre the reporte thereof to other that know more. (Holin. 1577, 2:1765r)

Fleming, whose hostility toward Mary is one of the hallmarks of his history of her reign, adds to Holinshed's list of possibilities an eyewitness account lifted directly from Foxe's *Acts and Monuments* (Foxe 7:126):

There came to me, whome I did both heare and see, one Isabel Malt, a woman dwelling in Aldersgate street in Horne allie, not farre from the house where this present booke was printed, who before witnesse made this declaration unto us, that she being delivered of a man-child upon Whitsundaie in the morning [the supposed time of Mary's delivery], which was the eleventh day of June Anno 1555, there came to hir the lord North, and another lord to hir unknowne, dwelling then about old Fish-street, demanding of hir if she would part with hir child, and would sweare that she never knew nor had no such child. Which if she would, hir sonne (they saide) should be well provided for, she should take no care for it, with manie faire offers if she would part with the child.
    After that came other women also, of whome one (she saide) should have been the rocker: but she in no wise would let go hir sonne, who at the writing hereof being alive and called Timothie Malt, was of the age of thirteene yeares and upward. Thus much (I saie) I heard of the woman hir self. What credit is to be given to her relation, I deale not withall, but leave it to the libertie of the reader, to beleeve it they that list: to them that list not, I have no futher warrant to assure them. (*Chronicles*, 4:82–83)

Foxe's anecdote is not unique in its claims that Mary's pregnancy was a hoax and that a substitution was plotted. Alice Perwick of London was indicted for claiming that "[t]he Queen's Grace is not with child, and another lady should be with child and that lady's child when she is brought in bed should be named the Queen's child."[4] Fleming's decision to include this scurrilous story functions on both a literal and a symbolic level. Not only does it contribute to his unflattering portrait of Mary, it also illustrates the sterility and death associated with Mary's reign. The failed promise of Mary's pregnancy evokes the failures, both political and religious, of her government, and the attempts to substitute another child for the royal heir suggests her substitution of the Roman church for England's true one.
    The transition between Mary's and Elizabeth's reigns also offers a telling example of the two authors' different approaches to their subject matter. In the 1577 edition, Holinshed concludes his narrative of Mary's monarchy and begins that of Elizabeth's without comment on either queen. Such potentially explosive subject matter as the execution of the Oxford martyrs for heresy is presented factually and impartially among

the lives and deaths of notable Catholics and Protestants who lived during Mary's reign. After depicting Mary Tudor's illness and death and summarizing her reign, Holinshed passes directly to Elizabeth's accession. The 1587 edition presents this transition quite differently. Fleming expands Holinshed's original four paragraphs concluding Mary's reign to 18 and adds such comments as "More English bloud spilled in queene Marie's time, than ever was in anie king's reigne before hir," and "Queene Marie never had good successe in anie thing she went about"(*Chronicles,* 4:138). In the 1587 edition, the chapter ends with a declaration in large italic type: "Thus farre the troublesome reigne of Queene Marie the first of that name (God grant she may be the last of hir religion) eldest daughter to king Henrie the eight" (4:159). The new chapter heralds Elizabeth's reign with even larger type, "The peaceable and prosperous regiment of blessed Queene Elisabeth, second daughter to king Henrie the eight," and adds the following paragraph before returning to the original 1577 text: "After all the stormie, tempestuous, and blustering windie weather of queene Marie was overblowne, the darkesome clouds, of discomfort dispersed, the palpable fogs and mists of most intollerable miserie consumed, and the dashing showers of persecution overpast: it pleased God to send England a calme and quiet season, a cleare and lovelie sunshine, a quitset from former broiles, of a turbulent estate, and a world of blessings by good queene Elisabeth: into whose gratious reigne we are now to make an happie entrance as followeth" (4:155). Holinshed's factual record is displaced by Fleming's vociferous rhetoric in the 1587 edition, and the emphasis moves from the actual events to their political implications for England.

As a history, Holinshed's 1577 "Historie of England" is far more sophisticated a narrative than it has been given credit for being. Although at times the sheer bulk of information overwhelms its purpose, the text has a clear focus and point of view. Holinshed states a distinct reason for including the numerous sources, and his accumulation of material is not the result of carelessness or naïveté but a conscious effort to preserve and pass on all of England's historical heritage. While he presents parallel and occasionally contradictory sources, he does not leave his readers entirely to their own devices to interpret and evaluate these materials but often attempts to shape their response through commentary or asides. Throughout his text he draws political lessons from history, demonstrating the importance of a unified and strong England in which both monarch and subject, adhering to their duties and responsibilities, preserve the health of the commonwealth. Unfortunately, very few scholars will ever read Raphael Holinshed's "Historie of England" because it has never been reprinted in a modern edition. It is Fleming's and not Holinshed's history that we read now, although Holinshed bears the dubious privilege of having his name attached to the text.

The 1587 "Historie of England"

Holinshed has borne much of the blame for the weaknesses of the "Historie of England," such as its virulent Protestant polemics, poor organization, and inclusion of extraneous material, but these elements can all be credited to Abraham Fleming's revisions and characterize the 1587, not the 1577, edition. The textual revisions that appear in the 1587 "Historie of England" are extensive, including not only the addition of material but also the deletion and rewriting of the existing contents. Some of these changes were smoothly incorporated into the history without detracting from its narrative continuity, but more often than not, moral commentary, extensive tangential digressions, catalogues, and ephemera were inserted into the history with no particular attention paid to textual transitions or organization.

Not all of Fleming's revisions detracted from the "Historie of England." Fleming incorporated a number of editorial changes that actually made the history easier to read. The only organizing principle that Holinshed had used in the 1577 English history was the arrangement of material by the reigns of monarchs. Fleming preserved Holinshed's chronological sequence for the English history before 1066 but divided the immense amount of material into eight books, subdivided the books into chapters, and then introduced each chapter with an extensive title summarizing the contents. Editorial revisions found throughout the entire history include headings that list both the chronological year and the year of each monarch's reign, extensive indexes, cross-references within the text, expanded marginalia acknowledging sources, quotation marks to indicate direct speech, and paragraph markers. The paragraph markers serve a variety of functions: to indicate a change in topic, a digression, an aside, or a commentary on the narrative; to indicate a change of author; and to indicate an insertion by Fleming, although he does not mark all his revisions in this manner. Other minor editorial changes include the use of Gothic rather than italic print for the marginalia, minor spelling revisions, and the setting off of longer speeches through quotations or subheadings.

The "Historie of England" before the Norman Conquest remained essentially unchanged in content. From the time of the Norman Conquest through Elizabeth's reign, Fleming added extensive material, including more information and lengthy digressions. He also expanded the history that he inherited from Holinshed with copious marginal notes, Latin aphorisms and poems, extensive references to and commentary on natural wonders such as eclipses, floods, earthquakes, and comets, and numerous anecdotes borrowed from Hall's *Union,* Foxe's *Acts and Monuments,* John Stow's *Historie of England,* and other sources.

Fleming's outspoken commentary is probably the one element most responsible for the English history's change in tone from objective to polemical. These comments are primarily, but not solely, religious in nature. Some of them are additions to the main body of the text, such as the condemnation of Thomas à Becket's life after the narrative of his murder. Anti-Catholic comments also occur in the marginalia criticizing the Catholic viewpoint of the history's many monastic sources. For example, in the marginalia accompanying the depiction of Henry II's reconciliation with the Church after Thomas à Becket's murder, Fleming states, "O vile subjection unbeseeming a king!" (*Chronicles,* 2:143), and in the narrative of John I's struggles with Rome he sets off the papal legate's speech to John with the subtitle "The sawcie speech of proud Pandulph the popes lewd legat, to king John, in the presumptuous popes behalfe" (2:306). Fleming advises the reader to "Note the ungodlie life of these catholikes" (4:136) and refers to the pope as "their hellish . . . father" (2:147).

A number of Fleming's moralizing comments accompany reports of calamity or death and warn of fortune's transitory nature, such as the following meditation that he includes after his account of the Duke of Norfolk's death:

> This was the ende of the Duke of Northfolke, a man whose life God had limited, as also the estate wherein he sometimes flourished: both which (as all things else) in a short time vanished. Let all degrees therefore learne, both by precept and example to know God principallie, secondlie their sovereigne Gods annointed, and finallie themselves to be subjects: forgetting their owne honour, which puffeth men up manie times with the wind of vainglorie, even to their owne overthrow, whilest they become insolent, and dreame that the transitorie advancements of this world will make them princes; princes peeres, naie (O monstrous madnesse) gods, whereas all things are mutable and momentarie, and the

higher that a man dooth clime, the greater is his fall. (*Chronicles,* 4:
269–70)

Other passages, attached to accounts of rebellion or treason, warn of the
consequences of such acts, for both the individual and the community.
In a moralizing insert added to the account of the War of the Roses during Henry VI's reign, Fleming notes:

> Thus you see what fruits the tree of civill discord dooth bring foorth; that
> evill tree, which whilest some have taken paine to plant, and some to
> proine and nourish, for others confusion (to whome they have given a
> taste of those apples which it bare, far more bitter than coloquintida)
> themselves have beene forced to take such share as befell them by lot. For
> as it is not possible that a comon fier, whose heat & flame is universallie
> spread, should spare any particular place (for so should it not be generall)
> no more is it likelie that in civill commotions, rebellions, insurrections,
> and partakings in conflicts and pitched feelds (speciallie under ring-
> leaders of great countenance and personage, such as be the peeres and
> states of kingdoms) anie one should, though perhaps his life, yet (a thou-
> sand to one) not save his bloud unspilt, nor his goods unspoiled. (*Chroni-
> cles,* 3:261)

In his condemnation of civil discord, Fleming follows Holinshed but
adds even more detailed moralizing to his depiction of events.

Fleming also includes numerous accounts of omens, dreams, and portents along with extended commentary explaining their significance.
Holinshed had included these elements in the 1577 edition but not to
the same degree, and his presentation of such phenomena was not mor-
alized. Fleming's additions usually carry a moralizing gloss overtly
explaining the significance of such wonders. Throughout the narrative,
he asserts their importance and defends their inclusion: "[P]rodigious
woonders, and other rare and unaccustomed accidents are significations
of some notable event insuing, either to some great personage, to the
common-wealth, or to the state of the church. And therfore it is a matter woorth the marking, to compare effects following with signes and
woonders before going; since they have a doctrine in them of no small
importance" (*Chronicles,* 2:178). Fleming also elaborates upon preexist-
ing narratives concerning bizarre phenomena. For example, to Holinshed's straightforward anecdote of "a fish like to a man," which was
brought up in a net during the reign of John I, Fleming adds, "Which
report of theirs in respect to the strangenesse thereof might seeme

incredible, speciallie to such as be hard of beleefe, and refuse to give faith and credit to anything but what their owne eies have sealed to their consciences, so that the reading of such woonders as these, is no more beneficiall to them, than to carrie a candle before a blind man, or to sing a song to him that is starke deafe. Nevertheless, of all uncouth and rare sights, speciallie of monstruous appearances we ought to be so farre from having little regard; that we should rather in them and by them observe the event and falling out of some future thing, no lesse miraculous in the issue, than they be woonderfull at the sudden sight" (2:290–91). Not all of the 1587 additions concerning portents and other wonders can be attributed to Fleming, for John Stow, who also contributed to the later English history, was fascinated by such events and included a number of them in his additions to the text. Stow, unlike Fleming, refrained from moralizing on their significance, and so his contributions in this area can usually be distinguished from Fleming's.

While Fleming's contributions form the bulk of the material added to the 1587 "Historie of England," writers whose major work appeared in other parts of the *Chronicles* supplied material as well. John Hooker, who revised and continued the "Historie of Ireland," contributed the "Description of the Citie of Excester" and a history of Exeter cathedral. Francis Thynne, who revised and continued the "Historie of Scotland," contributed several unpublished antiquarian essays, all of which were later censored. John Stow's exact role in the 1587 "Historie of England" is difficult to ascertain. Stow had provided Holinshed with manuscripts and other sources for the 1577 history and contributed material such as the Earl of Leicester's activities in the Netherlands, accounts of the city of London, and a number of the bizarre events and portents mentioned previously, but the extent of his direct contributions remains unclear, as does his role in the "Continuation of the Historie of England," which extended the English history from 1577 to 1586 (Parry, 1987, 637–38; Dodson, 58).

The 1587 "Historie of England" employs ecclesiastical history as part of the teleological focus of its narrative, beginning with its depiction of the conflict between the native English church and the Roman church introduced by Augustine of Canterbury and continuing through various monarchs' quarrels with the clergy. Fleming's inclusions become far more prevalent from the time of the Norman kings, and as the history progresses, the struggle between church and state metamorphoses into one between king and clergy, and ultimately between England and Rome. Thus the entire English history becomes a precursor to

Henry VIII's break with Rome and the English Reformation. Fleming incorporates this greater emphasis on ecclesiastical history into the existing 1577 narrative through the inclusion of marginalia, anecdote, and commentary. Most of the material for these revisions came from John Foxe's *Acts and Monuments,* which is heavily cited in the margins of the text.

As Patterson notes, Holinshed and his successors turned to Foxe's *Acts and Monuments* for a source of material as well as for certain historiographical practices such as the salvage and preservation in print of early documents and the use of anecdote and eyewitness accounts (Patterson 1994, 37). While it is true, as Patterson claims, that Holinshed avoided Foxe's Protestant polemic for a more objective stance on religion and focused on political rather than church history, this is not the case in Fleming's 1587 revision. A number of critics have called Fleming's own Protestant polemics one of the defining features of the 1587 English history.[5] The influence of Foxe's *Acts and Monuments* on the 1587 "Historie of England" cannot be overemphasized. It provided not only a substantial amount of the new textual material and a historiographical method, but also an entire shift in tone and in focus. Fleming's modifications of the "Historie of England" exemplify Richard Helgerson's observation that "in early modern England the language of politics was most often the language of religion."[6] In the 1587 history the separation of the English church from the church of Rome becomes a major theme of the text, and much of the material borrowed from Foxe contributes to this reordering of focus.

Fleming includes numerous anecdotes from Foxe's *Acts and Monuments* throughout his history, but nowhere are they so evident as in his account of Mary Tudor's reign. Borrowed directly from Foxe, Fleming's accounts of the Duchess of Suffolk and Dr. Edwin Sands have an almost hagiographic quality. Both the duchess and Sands are persecuted by Mary for their religion, flee the authorities, suffer greatly, are almost captured, escape to the Continent through the kindness of others, and return to their friends and loved ones under Elizabeth's reign (*Chronicles,* 4:104–17). Fleming also follows Foxe in portraying Mary's imprisonment of Elizabeth as due to the princess's religious beliefs rather than for political reasons and Elizabeth's preservation from execution as witness to God's providential power (4:121). Fleming heightens the emotional impact of the Protestant persecutions by making them personal and immediate through the stories of these three and other individuals. Furthermore, by including Foxe's interpretation of Elizabeth's imprisonment, Fleming links the political and ecclesiastical histories of England by placing the lives of political figures within a religious context.

Elizabeth, identified with those who suffered for their faith, becomes one of those persecuted for Christ and therefore an exception to the usual portrait of monarchs as persecutors of the godly, since Elizabeth's imprisonment for religious beliefs revealed her to be one of the godly herself. In Foxe's *Acts and Monuments* religious persecution is a sign of the Antichrist, and any regime that exercises institutional violence in matters of religion is anti-Christian. Foxe always equated persecutors with the Antichrist and the persecuted with Christ (Helgerson, 259–61). Fleming's debt to Foxe in the 1587 "Historie of England" reveals why he strongly emphasizes in the later history of Elizabeth's reign that Edmund Campion and others were executed for treason, not religion. For Elizabeth and her government to engage in religious persecution would immediately identify her with the very practices that he had so soundly condemned in the reign of her predecessor, Mary. Fleming, in following Foxe's lead of presenting Elizabeth among those godly individuals persecuted for their faith and her reign as a period of Christian peace, had to claim that she did not engage in religious persecution.

The result of this emphasis on ecclesiastical as well as political history resulted in the transformation of the 1587 "Historie of England" from a chronicle depicting English history as a cyclical series of events to one that is teleological in character. The 1587 English history draws on Foxe's apocalyptic vision of history as a continuing struggle between the forces of God and Satan, of Christ and Antichrist, concluding in a triumphant final victory for Christ and his Church. In the 1577 history, Elizabeth's reign is treated as one in a series of reigns, and although the narrative of her regime may be longer than that of the preceding ones, this is only natural given the *Chronicles'* emphasis on contemporary affairs and eyewitness accounts. Although the importance of the English church's history is not emphasized in the 1577 edition, Fleming brings the church's history to the forefront through his additions to the text in the 1587 edition, many of which are religious in nature. Fleming turns the English history into a struggle between good and evil, one in which England's secular and religious histories are closely intertwined. England's struggle to free itself from foreign intervention is often presented within a religious context, with Rome portrayed as the most serious threat to English sovereignty, both secular and religious. In Fleming's 1587 revision, all England's history is a precursor to Elizabeth's monarchy, which then becomes the triumphant realization of England's secular and religious autonomy. Mary Tudor's reign in particular emphasizes this struggle, and Fleming portrays these years as the dark night of England's collective soul before the glorious sunshine of Elizabeth's reign.[7]

Fleming, like Foxe, depicts Elizabeth as a godly ruler who ends the persecution of the elect and institutes a period of peace and prosperity (Helgerson, 260). Her role as God's chosen one is emphasized from the very beginning. On Elizabeth's birth, Fleming claims, "From that time forward (God himselfe undertaking the tuition of this yoong princesse, having predestinated hir to the accomplishment of his divine purpose) she prospered under the Lords hand, as a chosen plant of his watering" (*Chronicles,* 3:787). In comparing Mary's and Elizabeth's reigns, he states, "[I]t is hard to saie, whether the realme of England felt more of Gods wrath in queene Maries time, or of Gods favour and mercie in these so blessed and peaceable daies of queene Elisabeth" (4:138). In Fleming's history, Elizabeth is providentially appointed as the restorer of the true faith in England, and her reign is blessed by God.

Although the narrative of Elizabeth's reign is the longest in the "Historie of England," it is the most incoherent and the weakest narratively. Most of the accounts of preceding monarchs, such as those of the Plantagenets and the early Tudors, were adapted from Hall. For Elizabeth's reign as well as for those of Edward VI and Mary, there is no master narrative, and therefore the accounts of their reigns are more chronicle-like, fragmented, and disorganized. Though this is not a serious problem in the narratives of Edward's and Mary's reigns, primarily because they are both so short, it does make the narrative almost incomprehensible in the parts of the history that deal with Elizabeth's reign.

Holinshed often compressed and streamlined the material that he gathered from his sources, focusing on action and often deleting extended description or dialogue. Fleming, who seems exceedingly interested in the details of pageants, processions, and other diversions, often reinserted this information in his 1587 revision. He seems particularly fascinated with descriptions of clothing and pomp, and many of his additions to the Tudor history focus on the lavish displays and pageants of the various monarchs' reigns. With the exception of Elizabeth's coronation ceremony, Holinshed tends to present brief relations of such events. For example, Holinshed summarizes Anne Boleyn's coronation in three paragraphs. Fleming, drawing from Hall, expands it with extravagant descriptions of her arrival at Westminster, the pageants presented in her honor, the clothing worn by all the participants in the event, the dinners, and the actual coronation ceremony. In the 1577 edition, Elizabeth's birth consists of one paragraph giving the date and time of her birth, the date of the christening, and the names of her godparents. Again drawing from Hall, Fleming gives a detailed description of the christening ceremony, the decorations in the church, the procession to the font, Elizabeth's christening clothes, and the various lavish gifts given her by her godparents.

Fleming's taste for the sensational and the shocking, to which he later gave full reign in the "Continuation" of the English history, is another noteworthy element of his 1587 revision. Again, his approach is strikingly different from that of Holinshed. In his account of Henry IV's reign, Holinshed refers to the Welshwomen's postbattle mutilation of dead enemies: "The shamefull villanie used by the Welshwomen towards the dead carcasses, was such, as honest eares would be ashamed to heare, and continent toongs to speake therof" (*Chronicles*, 3:20). Fleming obviously doesn't share Holinshed's delicacy concerning such tales, since a few pages later he includes an explicit account of the Welsh mutilation of corpses, defending his inclusion of the material by stating, "This was a verie ignominious deed, and a woorsse not committed among the barbarous: which though it make the reader to read it, and the hearer to heare it, ashamed: yet bicause it was a thing doone in open sight, and left testified in historie; I see little reason whie it should not be imparted in our mother toong to the knowledge of our owne countrimen, as well as unto strangers in a language unknown" (3:34). As in his defenses of his inclusion of portents, omens, and other examples of the bizarre or sensational, Fleming seems to anticipate censure for the material that he chose to include in the "Historie of England." Here and elsewhere, his insistence on his readers' right to information, no matter what its character, suggests that Fleming, even more so than Holinshed, was dedicated to creating as inclusive and multivocal a text as possible.

"The Continuation of the Historie of England," the 1587 update of the English history from 1577 to 1586, concerns those events of Elizabeth's reign that occurred after the publication of the 1577 *Chronicles*. Though it covers only half the time period (1576–1586) that the earlier narrative of Elizabeth's monarchy does (1558–1576), it is more than three times its length. The size of this section is due not so much to its wealth of historical information, but rather to the extensive inclusion of extraneous material such as Thynne's and Hooker's catalogues and the entire texts of royal grants, proclamations, confessions, pamphlets, speeches, entertainments, and masques. Consequently, the narrative is even more fragmented and disconnected than the earlier history of Elizabeth's regime.

Although the "Continuation" lists "John Stow and others" as the authors, textual evidence strongly suggests that Abraham Fleming was the primary author, and although Stow probably contributed substantially to the text, the actual extent of his participation is almost impossible to determine. It is fairly clear that the revision of the existing "Historie of England" was done by Fleming, since he tended to identify information that he obtained from other sources with such marginal notes as "Abraham Fleming from Edward Hall," "Abraham Fleming from John Foxe," or "Abraham Fleming from John Stow." Nearly all the new references to Stow in the 1587 history appear in this form. In the "Continuation," however, Stow's name rarely appears in the margin and never in this particular format (Dodson, 58). Fleming's claim to primary authorship is supported by the fact that he wrote and initialed the epistle at the beginning as well as the conclusion at the end of the history. The text's heavy moralizing and its focus on pageantry and entertainment as well as bizarre phenomena continue Fleming's inclusion of these elements in the revision of the 1577 history. Furthermore, the marginal notes are essentially the same in tone and sentiment as those that Fleming contributed to the revision of the existing "Historie of England." Fleming's contributions tend to be more thoroughly developed narratively and include a significant amount of analysis, whereas those contributions of Stow's that can be positively identified are characterized by their clearness of presentation and lack of moralizing. Stow's contributions also tend to follow the chronicle format more closely in that unrelated events appear in chronological order, without attention to their relative significance to the history as a whole. Because of this, the "Continuation" is the most typical example of the chronicle genre in the later English history (Dodson, 58).

The discretion and sober responsibility of Raphael Holinshed's narrative can be fully appreciated only when one contrasts the "Continuation" to the "Historie of England" as it appeared in 1577, or even as it appeared before 1576 in the 1587 edition, which, although expanded and revised, was still shaped by Holinshed's original format. The "Continuation" gives full reign to the sensationalist accounts of portents, disturbances of nature, murders, freak accidents, and violent executions that are scattered throughout, but do not dominate, the preceding portion of the English history. Deaths caused by catastrophes such as the collapse of a scaffold at the Bear Garden or the explosion of a gunpowder house in Fetter Lane occur with notable regularity throughout the text (*Chronicles,* 4:504–5). Castles and ships appear in the clouds; hailstorms rain stones shaped like frogs, mattocks, swords, and skulls; the ubiquitous blazing stars stream through the skies; and, as Fleming moralizes, a rash of monstrous births "signifieth our monstrous life, which God for his mercie give us grace to amend" (4:430–32). Despite Fleming's "Epistle's" reference to this period as "the golden reigne of blessed queene Elisabeth, the sweet floure of amiable virginitie," the ominousness of these incidents colors the historical events that are laid out in the text.

A steady parade of treason trials and executions balances Fleming's almost hysterical insistence on the intense adoration of Elizabeth's subjects for their monarch. Despite the detailed descriptions of the "Triumph of the Four Foster Children of Desire," presented in 1581 in Elizabeth's honor; of the 1582 festivities in honor of the departure of Elizabeth's final suitor, the Duke of Alençon; and of the queen's 1578 reception in Norwich, complete with an account of the citizens' communal melancholy "proceeding from the departure of hir highnes roiall person," the even more detailed descriptions of the trials and executions of Edmund Campion, Francis Throckmorton, William Parry, and the Babington conspirators are the defining feature of the "Continuation." As Annabel Patterson has noted, the contrast between official celebration and official violence becomes even more ironic given the absence of truly significant matters of national concern, such as the vocal opposition of Elizabeth's marriage to the Duke of Alençon or the anti-Whitgift campaign in the 1584 and 1586 Parliaments (Patterson 1994, 70).

The realization that his choice of topics might invite critical comment did not escape Abraham Fleming, who seems well aware that much of his material is better suited to the ballad sheet or pamphlet than to a serious history. He argues, "It were better to record the receiving of the queenes maiestie into Suffolke and Norffolke, than making no commemoration therof at all, to let it perish in three halfepenie pamphlets, and so die in oblivion" (*Chronicles,* 4:375). A similar defense, in which Fleming justifies the moral value of his material to later generations of readers, accompanies the account of two people's suffocation by fire: "Of this lamentable accident people talked diverslie, and pamphlets were published to make the same more knowne, howbeit, to leave the certeine meanes of the event to his knowledge that understandeth and seeth all things, let it be a warning to all ages so to live, as that an honest report may attend their death, and shame flie from them as a cloud before the wind" (4:504). The "Continuation" includes not only typical pamphlet material, but often the entire texts of the original pamphlets, as in the case of the Campion trial's narrative. Fleming's desire to conserve such historical trivia is certainly in keeping with the *Chronicles'* contributors' efforts to provide the most comprehensive history possible, yet at times it appears that the real reason for their inclusion, and indeed the inclusion of most events in the "Continuation," is their spectacular or sensationalist content.

The depiction of the various conspiracies, both real and imagined, against Elizabeth that constitute such a significant portion of the "Continuation" develop the underlying argument of the entire "Historie of England," that "[t]his little Iland, God having so bountifullie bestowed his blessings upon it, that except it proove false within it selfe, no treason whatsoever can prevaile against it" (*Chronicles,* 4:449). The "discovery" of these various conspiracies before they could be implemented and the presentation of the general population's joy over the conspirators' arrest, as in the case of the Babington plot, illustrate this declaration of providential care and civic unity. As in the earlier history, civil unrest and internal strife are portrayed as the greatest threats to England's well-being, and Fleming's presentation of an England united behind its queen suggests that these cases of treason were an anomaly, did not reflect popular opinion against Elizabeth, and were doomed to failure. Nevertheless, the sheer number of trials in this later portion of Elizabeth's reign create a certain ambiguity within the text. The "Historie of England" includes material presenting both the government's and the defendants' point of view in these trials' accounts, and authorial sympathy appears to lie with the forces of law and order, yet the inclusion of all voices relating to the trials as well as the steady stream of violence creates a narrative that undercuts and even contradicts the textual commentary.

Such is the case in the "Continuation's" account of Edmund Campion's trial, in which Elizabeth's government maintained that Campion had died a traitor's and not a martyr's death. Was Campion executed for treason or for his religion? As in the case of Matthew Hamont, a ploughwright who was executed in 1579 "for that he denied Christ our saviour" and "bicause he spake words of blasphemie (not to be recited) against the queenes majestie and others of hir councell," the distinction was not always clear (*Chronicles,* 4:405–6). Patterson has noted the interrelationship of political and religious repression during the latter half of Elizabeth's reign (Patterson 1994, 129). Under Elizabeth's "Act to Retain the Queen's Majesty's Subjects in their Due Obedience" (March 1581), which extended the treason law to cover anyone who withdrew subjects from their obedience either to the queen or to the Church of England, or who converted them "for that intent" to Roman Catholicism, treason and religious dissension would seem to be the same. Yet paradoxically, Campion's execution provoked a propaganda war in which Elizabeth's government seemed determined to prove they were not. In response to Catholic accusations both at home and abroad that Campion's only crime was his religion, Lord Burghley himself circulated two pamphlets, "The Execution of Justice in England for Maintenance of Publicke and Christian Peace, Against Certeine Stirrers of Sedition, and Adherents to the Traitors and Enemies of the Realme, without Anie Persecution of Them for Questions of Religion, As is Falslie Reported and Published by the Authors and Fosterers of Their Treason" and "A Declaration of the Favourable Dealing of Hir Majesties Commissioners Appointed for the Examination of Certeine Traitors, and of Tortures Unjustlie Reported to be Done Upon Them for Matters of Religion." "The Execution of Justice" appeared in December 1583 and "A Declaration" soon after. The entire texts of both pamphlets are included in the 1587 account of Campion's trial, as is the text of an official pamphlet read to Campion and his confederates at the place of execution, "An Advertisment and defence for truth against all backbiters and speciallie against the whispering favourers and colorers of Campions and the rest of his confederats treason." The inclusion of these texts would certainly imply that the chronicler's sympathies lay with the official version of the execution.

As Cyndia Clegg has noted, the *Chronicles'* report of Campion's trial exposed both sides of the issue to public scrutiny (Clegg 1997, 141). Not only official and officially sanctioned accounts, but also the accused men's pleas of innocence, including Campion's entire defense, as well as Catholic outcries against English justice, originally appeared in the *Chronicles'* account, although Fleming condemns these outcries as "libels" and "lying reports." His accounts of the miracles that supposedly occurred after Campion's execution are also framed by accusations of falsehood: "It was bruted abroad not by men, but brute beasts, that on the selfe same daie whereon Campion was executed, the river of Thams did neither eb nor flow, but stood still. O miracle! Whether this were a lie or not, as all the world may sweare it was no truth" (*Chronicles,* 4:460).

Ironically, Fleming's eagerness to refute the various claims of both injustice and miraculous events resulted in the censorship of not only those claims but of his refutations as well. For although the account of the three executions remains the same, including the accused men's protestations of innocence, in the censored 1587 *Chronicles,* Fleming's discussion of the aftermath of the executions was completely deleted. As both Anne Castanien and Clegg have pointed out, Fleming, in seeking to refute the claims of injustice and miracles associated with Campion's death, circulated the very information that Elizabeth's government wanted the public, both at home and abroad, to forget.[8]

Both the anecdote that opens the "Continuation" and the prayer that closes it are emblematic of the violence and internal strife that permeate the "Historie of England" and thus form a suitable conclusion to the whole. The opening narrative, provided by John Stow, evokes the story of the primal murder in its depiction of a man who treacherously killed his own sibling, thinking that his crime would remain hidden: "The tenth day of November, in the citie of Worcester, a cruell and unnaturall brother (as an other Cain) murdered his owne naturall and loving brother, first smiting his braines out of his head with an ax, and after cutting his throte to make him sure, and then buried him under the earth of a chimneie . . . but not long after this secret murder comming to light, the murderer was rewarded according to his deserts, and to the terror of such unnaturall murthering brethren" (*Chronicles,* 4:343). The unnaturalness of the act, its discovery and punishment, and the warning to all other "murthering brethren" become the paradigm for the events that follow in the "Conclusion." Fittingly, the last major incident to be recorded in its pages involves Parliament's petitions to execute Mary, Queen of Scots, for treason, Elizabeth's resistance, and her final sentence given against the Scottish queen. Abraham Fleming's concluding remarks to the "Continuation" draw one last link between treachery and family: "O Lord in vengeance give [them] the judgement of Judas, as they have beene partakers of his sinne; let them be intangled and taken in the traps of their trecheries, and swallowed up in the seas of deserved confusion, that they be no more a familie" (4:952). On 8 February, less than a month after the 1587 publication of Holinshed's *Chronicles,* Mary was executed for plotting the assassination of her cousin Elizabeth.

On 1 February 1587, about two weeks after its printing, the later edition of Holinshed's *Chronicles* was called in by the Privy Council concerning "matters of later yeers that concern the State." The Council directed John Whitgift, Archbishop of Canterbury, to halt further sale until the contents had been reviewed and reformed. The archbishop was to be assisted in the examination of the text by a committee composed of Thomas Randolph, Master of the Posts, a diplomat and trusted agent of the queen and Burghley; Henry Killigrew, also a diplomat and an advisor to the Earl of Leicester; and Dr. John Hammond, a member of the Court of High Commission, as well as any others he might think appropriate.[9]

The resulting corrections in the "Historie of England" excised Francis Thynne's "A Discourse of the Earls of Leicester," "A treatise of the Lords Cobham," "The Lives of the Archbishops of Canterbury," "A Catalogue of the Lord Wardens of the Cinque Ports," and a biography of all Scottish kings named James. Accounts of the execution of Edmund Campion; the departure of the Duke of Alençon for the Netherlands; Francis Drake's return from the Caribbean; the deaths of Henry, Mary, and Philip Sidney; the Earl of Leicester's first visit to the Netherlands; and the discovery, trial, and execution of the Babington conspirators were also severely revised and condensed.

One of the more noteworthy elements of the *Chronicles'* censorship is the lack of public records concerning any incidents of search, seizure, or punishment. No records exist of interviews with the transgressing publishers or authors or of the imposition of any penalties (Castanien, 12). Apparently, the expurgation took place without any incident, and the revisions appear to have been completed quickly.

Because of the lack of public records, the reasons behind the castration of the *Chronicles* remain unknown, although a number of theories have been advanced. Patterson believes that the Privy Council's fear that the uncensored text could produce the wrong sort of reaction among sections of the public led to the *Chronicles'* censorship (Patterson 1994, 234). Elizabeth Story Donno has argued that those passages relating to the Sidneys were excised because of the queen's hostility toward Sir Philip, stemming from his activities in the Netherlands, while those relating to the Earl of Leicester may have been motivated by the earl's own concern for his public reputation (Donno 1987, 239, 242–44). Castanien believes that a number of reasons existed for the various expurgations, depending on the particular site of censorship. Regarding the censorship of Campion's trial, she argues that Fleming, in seeking to refute the claims of injustice and miracles associated with Campion's death, circulated the very information that Elizabeth's government wanted the public to forget. The timing of this was particularly crucial, for although Campion had died five years earlier, at the time of the publication of the 1587 *Chronicles,* England was faced with a similarly awk-ward situation in the case of Mary, Queen of Scots (Castanien, 275 –78). She notes that those excisions relating to the Earl of Leicester's activities may have been ordered in response to the earl's own desire to reduce the emphasis on entertainment and make him seem more efficient and responsible as a military commander (271–72). On the other hand, G. J. R. Parry argues that the Earl of Leicester's 1586 campaign in the Netherlands may merely have been a casualty of the Privy Council's censorship of Francis Thynne's catalogue of the earls of Leicester, which indiscreetly emphasized their royal descent and political importance. Parry notes that most of John Stow's narrative concerning Leicester was reprinted and even expanded in his 1592 *Annals* and that it remained uncensored in that format. The removal of Thynne's catalogue involved a major revision of Stow's contribution, which Stow complained of later as being "left out through the evil dealing of some" (Parry, 1987b, 637–38). Clegg argues that the expurgations reveal a unifying theme in that they address the representation of English justice and law, and of England's respect for the sovereign rights of other countries. Clegg has also pointed out that the 1587 *Chronicles* was printed under royal privi-lege, suggesting that it enjoyed a status different from that of other texts censored by Elizabeth's government, and that its censorship and revision reflected the government's efforts to construct a favorable domestic and international image. Materials judged to jeopardize England's interna-tional image were ordered deleted or revised (Clegg 1997, 138).

For some excisions, no explanation seems possible except that they may have been casualties of the revision process, as Parry has argued in reference to Stow's account of the Earl of Leicester. The reviser's practice of removing whole sheets of paper rather than individual leaves may explain their removal. The revising editor appears to have compressed and modified the existing text to fit whatever sheets were reprinted, and some items may have been sacrificed in the process. Castanien has noted some of the material deleted from the *Chronicles* consists of apparently innocuous anecdotes that seem to pose no political problems, although these narratives may have had a contemporary significance lost to mod-ern readers (Castanien, 138 –39). As with the more politically volatile material that was censored, the continually shifting political climate that characterized Elizabeth's reign may have made unacceptable mate-rial that the *Chronicles'* authors had included in good faith.

The "Historie of England" held up to its English audience a mirror in which they could view themselves in terms of not only their contemporary situation but their historical past as well. It incorporated into a single narrative the traditions, legends, and facts that both molded and defined them as Englishmen. It gave them a sense of what it was to be English by depicting the common history that united them despite the divided religious and political loyalties that were driving them apart. As Richard Helgerson has stated, "Chronicle was the Ur-genre of national self-representation. More than any other discursive form, chronicle gave Tudor Englishmen a sense of their national identity" (Helgerson, 11). By supplying the means to interpret and evaluate their past, the "Historie of England" enabled its readers to discover for themselves the essence of that identity.

Chapter Three

The "Description of England"

William Harrison, who wrote the "Description of Scotland" as well as the "Description of England," stands alone as the single author from the 1577 *Chronicles* to contribute to the 1587 revision. Because Harrison was the only contributor to be involved in both editions, his "Description of England" is noteworthy as the one portion of Holinshed's *Chronicles* for which the author of the 1577 text revised and expanded his own work for the 1587 publication. Harrison's expansion and revision of his project offers a fascinating insight not only into his own development as a social observer, but into the various social and economic changes that took place in England between 1577 and 1587.

Although Harrison's "Description" was the most detailed and expansive example of the description genre to appear in England, it was not the first. Harrison drew on a tradition that had its roots in the work of the sixth-century monk Gildas and continued to develop through Ranulf Higden's fourteenth-century *Polychronicon*. In these texts, a topographical description preceded a chronological history, as Harrison's "Description" precedes Holinshed's "History" (Edelen 1968, xvi–xvii). Harrison's lists of islands, roads and highways, lakes and streams, cities, shires, and bishoprics come from this medieval tradition, which, in the absence of reliable maps, employed words to describe the geographical landscape.[1] Like the work of his predecessors, Harrison's text contains descriptions of England's topography, physical resources, climate, flora, and fauna as well as the customs and social organization of its human population. Harrison's "Description," however, ranges far beyond its antecedents in its extensive inclusion and richness of detail, providing a comprehensive view of English life in the late sixteenth century.

The "Description" is divided into three books, although the logic of the division is not always clear. In the 1577 edition, all three books are referred to as the "Description of Britain." In its final 1587 form, the first book is labeled the "Description of Britain" and the second two books the "Description of England." The first book provides details of England's physical and political geography, legends of its origin, histories of its language and religious belief, a portrait of its inhabitants, and a brief perusal of its most notable marvels. Harrison's attention to detail in the topographical sections of the first book is exhaustive. He devotes one lengthy chapter to more than three hundred offshore islands surrounding Great Britain. In chapters 11 through 16 he traces the courses of more than a thousand rivers and their tributaries, naming the parishes through which they flow and locating five thousand villages in doing so. Even chapter 17, "Of such ports and creeks as our sea-faring men doo note for their benefit upon the coasts of England," contains a list of more than two hundred of these waterways, although Harrison laments that he was not able to provide the same detailed descriptions for these that accompanied his rivers; it appears that his source notes had mysteriously disappeared.

Most of Harrison's historical information also appears in the first book. The chapters, "Of the ancient denominations of this Iland," "What sundrie nations have dwelled in Albion," "Of the languages spoken in this Iland," "The names of such kings and princes as have reigned in this Iland," and "Of the ancient religion used in Albion " contain the same mix of fact, legend, and fantasy typical of the historical descriptions of his time. For example, his chapter on the various inhabitants of Britain includes everyone from the mythical giant Albion and Brut the Trojan through the historical Saxons, Danes, and Normans, while his catalogue of the kings and princes of Britain claims to list every monarch from Samothes, the grandson of Noah, through Elizabeth Tudor.

The second book is even less clear in its organization, although the main emphasis appears to be English social customs, community life, and architecture. Much of the material on English society that appears in the 1587 edition of this book originally appeared in the third book of the 1577 edition. Harrison emphasizes the social conditions of his time by giving them a more prominent place in his later text. The transfer of this information from the third book to the second book also results in greater cohesiveness for the two sections, although a number of tangential chapters still appear in both. The second book includes chapters on England's churches and universities, legal system, class hierarchies, navy, munitions, and monetary system and the dress and dietary customs of its population. Descriptions of English architecture, cities and towns, fairs and markets, parks, gardens, and orchards also make up a significant portion of this section of the text. It is no surprise, given the social emphasis of the second book, that most of Harrison's 1587 social commentary appears here. As a source of information on life in sixteenth-century England, Harrison's second book is indispensable; it is still considered an essential text by scholars of the period.

Harrison's removal of English social customs from the 1587 third book resulted in a section focused primarily on the animal and mineral resources of England. Because of this, it is probably the most unified of the three books that make up the "Description." Even so, the book contains its share of tangential chapters, such as chapter 8, which advocates increased saffron production in England; a chapter on the English manner of counting time (as if it were much different from anyone else's); an additional chapter on fairs and markets, this one listing their dates and locations; and a final chapter on inns and thoroughfares, consisting primarily of a table listing the number of miles between various cities and towns. Harrison's English chauvinism manifests itself in his enthusiastic celebration of Britain's resources, although he admits his contemporaries do not seem to share his appreciation of England's abundant native wealth: "[F]or desire of noveltie, we oft exchange our finest cloth, corne, tin, and woolles, for. . . . painted feathers, gewgaws for fooles . . . and such like trumperie, whereby we reape just mockage and reproch in other countries" (*Chronicles,* 1:395).

While much of the "Description" is drawn from Harrison's personal experience, his topographical information comes from other sources, primarily John Leland's work. During Henry VIII's reign, Leland had been granted a commission to travel throughout England and Wales to undertake antiquarian research. He spent six years (about 1535–1543) traveling and making copious geographical and historical notes that included not only his own observations but also historical and genealogical information taken from local libraries and records. His goal was to compose maps of England and Wales and to accompany the maps with detailed geographical descriptions. Unfortunately, Leland died in 1552 after suffering a period of mental illness and was never able to organize his research. Even though they remained unorganized and unpublished until 1710, Leland's notes were a major source for a number of sixteenth- and seventeenth-century chronicles and other historical or topographical works, among them John Stow's *Survey of London,* William Camden's *Britannia,* William Lambard's *Perambulation of Kent,* Michael Drayton's *Poly-Olbion,* and Harrison's "Description of England."[2]

Though he continually reiterated his debt to Leland, Harrison also complained bitterly of the difficulty of working with the antiquarian's notes, which he describes as "motheaten, mouldie, & rotten . . . so confounded, as no man can (in a maner) picke out anie sense from them by a leafe togither"(*Chronicles,* 1:108–9). Harrison, as he admits to his patron, William Brooke, Lord Cobham, in his "Epistle Dedicatorie," had little choice but to rely on Leland given his own lack of knowledge: "I have not by my owne travell and eysight viewed such things as I doo here intreat of. In deed I must needs confesse, that untill now of late, except it were from the parish where I dwell, unto you Honour in Kent; or out of London where I was borne, unto Oxford and Cambridge where I have bene brought up, I never travelled 40. miles foorthright and at one journey in all my life" (1:vi). Harrison does not rely solely on Leland for his topographical data, however. He often compares Leland's notes to other material, and, as is the case in most of Holinshed's *Chronicles,* includes two or more sources if he can, inviting his readers to evaluate the information for themselves. For example, in describing the river Lune, he refers to two sources, "The first being set downe by Leland, as master Moore of Catherine hall in Cambridge delivered it unto him. The next I exhibit as it was given unto me, by one that hath taken paines (as he saith) to search out and view the same, but verie latelie to speake of." At the end of the two descriptions, Harrison advises his reader, "Thus have you both the descriptions of Lune, make your conference or election at your pleasure, for I am sworne to neither of them both" (1:145). Harrison tends to accumulate rather than synthesize topographical information, as when in concluding Leland's description of the river Witham, he adds, "Thus have I brieflie dispatched this noble river Witham. But having another note delivered me thereof from a freend, I will yeeld so farre unto his gratification, that I will remember his travell here, and set downe also what he hath written thereof, although the river be sufficiently described alredie" (1:170). Harrison thus sought to counter his own lack of geographical knowledge by supplying as many references as he possibly could.

From Leland's notes, Harrison drew not only his topographical information but his chapters on archaeology, metals, quarries, and salt mining as well. He often supplements or corrects details from Leland's notes with other primary sources—both ancient, such as Plutarch and Ptolemy, and modern, such as Christopher Saxton's recently completed maps, which he refers to as "Master Seckford's cards."[3] Harrison relied on John Stow's almanacs for the lists of fairs and markets, itineraries, and law terms. He drew on his own experiences as well as those of his neighbors and friends for his material on social classes, food, clothing, housing, furnishings, fairs, markets, inns, farming, housekeeping, and

gardening. Harrison lists his various sources and the manner in which he
evaluated and employed them in his "Epistle Dedicatorie:"

> One helpe and none of the smallest that I obtained herein, was by succh
> commentaries as *Leland* had sometime collected of the state of Britaine,
> books utterlie mangled, defaced with wet and weather, and finallie
> unperfect through want of sundrie volumes: secondlie, I gat some knowl-
> edge of things by letters and pamphlets, from sundrie places & shires of
> England, but so discordant now and then amongst themselves, especial-
> lie the names and courses of rivers and situation of townes, that I had oft
> greater trouble to reconcile them one with another, than orderlie to pen
> the whole discourse of such points as they contained: the third aid did
> grow by conference with divers, either at the table or secretlie alone,
> wherein I marked in what things the talkers did agree, and wherin they
> inpugned ech other, choosing in the end the former, and rejecting the
> later, as one desirous to set foorth the truth absolutelie, or such things in
> deed as were most likelie to be true. The last comfort arose by mine owne
> reading of such writers as have heretofore made mention of the condition
> of our countrie. (*Chronicles*, 1:vi)

Harrison's employment of popular and oral material as well as of scholarly information lends an immediacy and vibrancy to the narrative of
the "Description." Throughout the text, he often mentions gathering
information from friends, neighbors, and acquaintances as well as from
his own observations. Much of the text's interest comes from Harrison's
incorporation of these eyewitness accounts into his portrait of England's
national life.

Despite the array of sources mentioned in his dedication, it appears
from his comments in the 1577 "Description" that Harrison received far
less information than he had expected for this first edition. Apparently,
he did not have access to Christopher Saxton's maps until he had already
completed the first book, which contained most of his topographical
information.[4] This probably accounts for the appearance of topographical information in both the first book and the second book of the 1577
edition, and for Harrison's decision to rearrange it all into the first book
of the 1587 edition. Harrison also complains of being promised materials and other help that never arrived. Lacking "instruction, which hath
beene largelye promised, and slackly performed, and other sodayne and
injurious denyall of helpe voluntarily offred, wythout occasion gyven on
my part," he had to content himself with a "mangled rehearsall of the
residue" from his own knowledge and whatever sources he could find

(Holin. 1577, 1:19r.) He writes that although he had hoped to provide a complete picture of the "number, situation, names, quantities, townes, villages, castels, mounteines, fresh waters, plashes or lakes, salt waters" and other elements of the islands surrounding Britain, and had hoped "to have made a perfect description" of the "heads, courses, length, bredth, depth of Chanell (for burden) ebbes, flowinges, and falles" of British rivers, he was frustrated in his aspirations, having to rely upon Leland's haphazard notes and occasionally incomplete information (1:19r, 25r).

Besides the lack of resources, Harrison also struggled with a lack of time in his completion of the 1577 "Description": "For such was my shortnesse of time allowed in the writing, & so great the speede made in the Printing, that I could seldome with any deliberation peruse, or almost with any judgement deliberate exactly upon such notes as were to be inserted" (Holin. 1577, 1:sign.*2v.). It appears that the 1577 "Description" was written during a fairly short period in 1576 while Harrison was working on his *Chronology,* and that he had first declined to write the "Description" for fear that "the dealing therin might proove an impechement unto mine own Treatize" (1:sign.*2r). He refers to the "Description" as the "cromes" (crumbs) that "fell out" from his labors on the *Chronology.* Ironically, Harrison's *Chronology* was never published, and the crumbs have become his most famous work.

1577 and 1587

As the only one of the three "Descriptions" to undergo any revision for the updated *Chronicles,* Harrison's 1587 "Description" bears only a surface resemblance to its 1577 predecessor in content, focus, and especially tone. While some revisions consist simply of the insertion of words or phrases to clarify existing material, more significant structural changes include the deletion of some chapters, the addition of others, and the rearrangement of many of the remaining ones. For example, in the 1577 "Description," the first book contains three chapters on rivers, as does the second book. In the 1587 "Description," Harrison moved all six river chapters to the first book and divided the second book's chapter on the church of England into two, one on "the ancient and present state of the church of England" and the other on "the bishoprikes and their severall circuits." He moved his chapter on the marvels of England from the second book to the end of the first book, and, as mentioned earlier, he transferred all chapters on English social life from the second

book to the third book. Harrison added new accounts of such topics as
ancient navies, fashions in beards, English inns, the brewing of beer, and
gardens. He excised four chapters on weights and measures and added
new chapters on Parliament, ports and creeks, gardens and orchards,
British monarchs, and the division of the earth.

G. J. R. Parry claims that most of the major 1587 revisions are due to
the fact that Harrison had more time to research and write while working on the later edition, and because it appears that he was planning to
incorporate the expanded and updated "Description" into his own mas-
sive *Chronology*, the changes were probably made with that in mind
(Parry 1984, 809). To the 1587 edition Harrison added numerous classical allusions and quotations, as well as many historical parallels between
his own time and earlier ones. For example, in a 1587 attack on usury,
he draws on several classical references, including Cicero, Demosthenes,
and Athenaeus. To the chapter "Of parks and warrens," a discussion of
the evils of the enclosure system, he adds an example of similar greed in
classical Rome that he draws from Livy and closes the chapter with the
historical parallel of King John, whom he claims overthrew a number of
enclosures in 1209, "For hearing . . . by complaint of the countrie, how
these inclosures were the cheefe decaie of men, and of tillage in the land,
he sware with an oth that he would not suffer wild beasts to feed upon
the fat of his soile, and see the people perish for want of abilitie to procure and buie them food that should defend the realme"(*Chronicles*,
1:345). Obviously, in the 1587 "Description," Harrison was able to
evaluate and analyze his subject matter at more leisure, incorporating
classical and historical sources in a manner that would reinforce his
arguments. The addition of such references supports Parry's view that in
revising his "Description," Harrison finally had the time and resources
to compose the text that he had really wanted to write.

As Annabel Patterson has noted, the "Description" also includes a
marked transformation in tone between 1577 and 1587, revealing "a
darker view of the state of England in its entirety" (Patterson 1994, 68).
Patterson credits this transformation to the social and economic changes
taking place in England during this period. The differences between the
1577 version and the 1587 version of the chapter "Of the maner of
building and furniture of our houses" well illustrates Patterson's point.
The 1577 edition delineates the significant improvement in the standard of living in the second half of the sixteenth century, as observed by
"old men yet dwelling" in Harrison's village. These improvements
included "the multitude of chimnies lately erected," "the great amend-

ment of lodging," and "the exchange of treene platters into pewter, and wooden spoons into silver or tin" (Holin. 1577, 1:85v). Though Harrison acknowledges that "all things are growen to most excessive prices," he points to a significant increase in material wealth, even among "the inferiour Artificers and most fermers, who have learned also to garnish their cubbords with plate, their beddes with tapistrie, and silke hanginges, and their tables with fine naperie." Harrison attributes these improvements to God, who "hath blessed us with hys good giftes" (1:85r). In the 1587 edition, Harrison's appraisal of the benefits of the new economic order isn't quite so unequivocal. He changes a number of modifying adjectives to demonstrate that the improvement in the standard of living delineated in the 1577 edition was not as widespread as he had first presented it. For example, the "most farmers" of 1577 becomes the "many farmers" in the later edition, and "the great amendment of lodging" is qualified by the addition of the phrase "but not general." After noting the increased economic wealth of the artificers and farmers, Harrison adds, "who by vertue of their old and not their new leases for the most part learned also to garnish their cupboards" in reference to the farmers, thus alluding to the exorbitant increases in rents that were starting to drive many small husbandmen off the land. He also includes a list of three negative economic developments to balance the three positive ones that he first introduced in 1577: "the inhansing of rents," "the dailie oppression of copiholders, whose lords seeke to bring their poore tenants almost into plaine servitude and miserie," and usury, "now perfectlie practised almost by everie christian, and so commonlie that he is accompted but for a foole that dooth lend his monie for nothing"(*Chronicles*, 1:318). Harrison's three negative examples clearly point to the increased polarization between rich and poor and the growing concentration of wealth into fewer and fewer hands (Patterson 1994, 61–65).

The Purpose of Revision

Both Parry and Patterson make valid arguments as to the motives for revision of the 1587 "Description." The addition of classical and historical references to the text, extra chapters, and factual information would have required library research and the leisure to analyze and synthesize sources, a leisure that in the 1577 edition Harrison often complains he lacks. On the other hand, Harrison's social criticism, which often takes the form of short commentary or asides and which relied primarily on his own observations and evaluation of others' experience, certainly did not need extensive research or library sources. In fact, the 1577 edition contains its share of critical comments, directed primarily at the enclosure system, the hoarding of grain, and the deceitful nature of merchants.

The 1587 "Description" is markedly more cynical and critical than its predecessor. At times Harrison's commentary becomes a jeremiad, lamenting the decline in English morality and the increase in greed and corruption. It would be easy to dismiss Harrison as a provincial crank whose vision was as limited as his range of reference, except that the concerns he articulates reveal a prescient understanding of the increased economic misery and social polarization that was to become a fixture of English life for the next half decade.[5] The widening gap between rich and poor, the exploitation of the wage laborer and poor husbandman, the decline of a sense of social obligation in the gentry, the corruption of church and state, and the placing of individual advancement over the good of the commonwealth consistently reoccur as major themes in the 1587 "Description."

As Keith Wrightson has noted, the years between 1580 and 1630 signaled a period of gathering crisis marked by population expansion, long-term inflation of prices, increased rents, and a series of catastrophic harvest failures (Wrightson, 142–43). The demands of urban food markets also created increasing pressure on rural communities as they were drawn more deeply into integrated regional economies centered on the cities. Food production became focused more on these distant markets and less on local need.

Although the 1577 "Description" contains its share of complaints about these trends, the criticism is more frequent and extensive in the 1587 text. Harrison may have been born and raised in London, but his chief sympathy lay with the agrarian communities in which he spent his adult years. His responses to the social and economic changes of the late sixteenth century consistently underscore this rural point of view. He regarded most of the economic changes of the 1580s with great distrust, bitterly complaining of the disappearance of the self-sufficient local economies and the rise in larger, specialized farms designed to supply the urban markets: "If it were enacted that each one should keepe his next market with his graine, and not to run six, eight, ten, fourteene, or twentie miles from home to sell his corne, where he dooth find the highest price and therby leaveth his neighbors unfurnished, I doo not thinke but that our markets wold be farre better served than at this present they are"(*Chronicles,* 1:342). He was particularly resentful of market middlemen and complained that the country was "pestered with purveyors, who take up eggs, butter, cheese, pigs, capons, hens, chickens, hogs, bacon, etc., in one market . . . and suffer their wives to sell the same in another or to poulterers of London" (1:341). In the 1587 "Description," food becomes a metaphor for power. Those who control food, who hoard food, and who distribute food become the purveyors of power, deciding who shall eat and who shall not, who can pay and who cannot. Harrison portrays scarcity as the result of human greed and corruption, not crop failure. In the 1587 "Description," food, like power, becomes redistributed to urban centers, and Harrison's complaints, whether of food scarcities, monopolies, or inflation, revolve around his realization of the rural countryside's growing economic marginalization.

Though his continual complaints about rising prices and the scarcity of foodstuffs reveal a certain amount of self-interest, Harrison demonstrates a keen understanding of the impact these economic changes had on his neighbors, especially the poorest ones:

> For albeit that there be much more ground eared now almost in everie place, than hath beene of late yeares, yet such a price of corne continueth in each towne and market without any just cause (except it be that landlords do get licences to carie corne out of the land onelie to keepe up the peeces for their owne private gaines and ruine of the commonwealth) that the artificer and poor laboring man, is not able to reach unto it, but is drivin to content himselfe with horsse-corne, I meane, beanses, peason, otes, tares and lintels: and therefore it is a true proverbe, and never so well verified as now, that hunger setteth his first foot into the horsse manger. If the world last a while after this rather: wheate and rie will be no graine for poore men to feed on, and some caterpillars there are that can saie so much alreadie. (*Chronicles,* 1:283)

The scarcity of food in a time of increasing prosperity is a theme that Harrison returns to time and time again. At numerous points throughout the text he mentions the hoarding of grain, pointing to it as a "cause of death and scarsitie in time of great abundance"(*Chronicles,* 1:339). The antithesis between these two states, that of greatest need and that of greatest surplus, form the cornerstone of his social criticism in the revised "Description."

Economics in England

Harrison also appears acutely aware of the socioeconomic trends of the late sixteenth century that brought about this social polarization, including the growing divergence in the living standards of rich and poor and a redistribution of wealth toward the upper levels of society. Although the real incomes of the gentry, the yeomanry, merchants, and skilled professionals expanded during this period, those of the poorer husbandmen, cottagers, and urban wage earners declined. The rural gentry and wealthier yeomen benefited from low labor costs as employers and from rising prices as large-scale producers. Others who benefited were the merchants of the urban elite who experienced a period of great prosperity, especially if they were involved in overseas trade. The increased wealth of the gentry and yeomanry resulted in a greater market for the services and manufactured goods provided by skilled urban artisans and professionals. On the other hand, population pressure and agrarian change produced an increase in the wage-dependent laboring population while inflation depressed real wages. Enclosure and the extinction of common rights deprived the rural poor of self-sufficiency. The nature of poverty itself underwent a radical change; in the fifteenth and early sixteenth centuries, poverty was usually the result of a specific misfortune: sickness, injury, old age, the death of a spouse or parent. By the end of the sixteenth century, the poor included not only the occasional victim of misfortune or old age but also a significant number of able-bodied adults, many of them full-time wage laborers hovering on the brink of destitution. In both the city and the country, a permanent underclass was developing, collectively referred to as "the poor" (Wrightson, 134–41).

Again, Harrison's response to these social trends reveals his strong identification with England's nonaristocratic rural population. Although the wealthier members of both the urban and rural populations tended to benefit from the economic changes taking place at this time, Harrison targets merchants, monopolists, and larger landowners for his most pointed criticism, blaming them for the increased impoverishment of the working poor. To Harrison, merchants are little more than parasites, responsible for raising the prices of goods at home by conveying them out of the country. He complains that their number "is so increased in these our daies, that their onelie maintenance is the cause of the exceeding prices of forreine wares, which otherwise when everie nation was permitted to bring in hir owne commodities, were farre better cheape and more plentifullie to be had. Of the want of our commodities here at home, by their great transportation of them into other countries, I speake not, sith the matter will easilie bewraie it selfe" (*Chronicles,* 1:274). He criticizes the greed of the large landowner, who "espying a further commodity in their commons, holds, and tenures, doth find such means as therby to wipe many out of their occupyings [livings] and turn the same unto his private gains." He notes how these landowners forced out the smaller husbandmen, through the "encroaching and joining of house to house and laying land to land" and how the result was that "the inhabitants of many places of our country are devoured and eaten up and their houses either altogether pulled down or suffered to decay by little and little" (1:325). His view of urban artisans is hardly more positive than that of merchants and large landowners. Noting their increased standard of living, he criticizes them for slovenly workmanship, arguing that although their product may be "never more fine and curious to the eie, so was it never lesse strong and substantiall for continuance and benefit of the buiers" (1:276). He accuses artisans of trying to make a greater profit by investing less time and care in their wares. Harrison's strongest objections to the economic practices of these particular classes revolve around his perception of how they set individual economic well-being above the common good and increase their personal wealth to the detriment of their neighbors.

On the other hand, the yeoman farmers as he describes them are ideal citizens, whose prosperity results from hard work and thriftiness rather than the exploitation of market conditions. Although this may have not necessarily been the case, it was less likely that the yeoman farmer had the means to profit to the same degree as the larger landowner; neither was he as likely to exploit the poor husbandman. He would also have lived on his farm and been responsible for his own farming rather than relying solely on the labor of others, a point made in Harrison's portrait:

> with grasing, frequenting of markets, and keeping of servants (not idle servants as the gentlemen doo, but such as get both their owne and part of their masters living) [they] do come to great welth, in so much that manie of them are able and doo buie the lands of unthriftie gentlemen . . . And albeit they be not called master as gentlemen are, or sir as to knights apperteineth, but onelie John and Thomas, & c: yet have they beene found to have doone verie good service: and the kings of England in foughten battels, were woont to remaine among them . . . the prince thereby shewing where his chiefe strength did consist. (*Chronicles*, 1:275)

In this passage and elsewhere, Harrison depicts the yeoman farmer as the backbone of English society and of England's economy. His praise of this specific social class forms an interesting counterpoint to his pointed criticism of others.

Despite his concern over the increased impoverishment of the rural lower classes, Harrison's views concerning the poor tend to be fairly conservative. He distinguishes between the "deserving" and the "undeserving" poor, reserving his sympathy for the "settled poor," who had a place in society and were eligible for parish relief under Elizabethan Poor Laws. The "vagrant poor," displaced persons who wandered aimlessly throughout the countryside and were subject to considerable harassment by the authorities, he dismisses as criminals:

> With us the poore is commonlie divided into three sorts, so that some are poore by impotencie, as the fatherlesse child, the aged, blind and lame, and the diseased person that is judged to be incurable: the second are poore by casualtie, as the wounded soldier, the decaied householder, and the sicke person visited with grievous and painefull diseases: the third consisteth of thriftlesse poore, as the riotour that hath consumed all, the vagabund that will abide no where, but runneth up and downe from place to place . . . and finallie the roge and the strumpet . . . For the first two sorts, that is to saie, the poore by impotencie, and the poore by casualtie, which are the true poore in deed, and for whome the word dooth bind us to make some dailie provision: there is order taken through out every parish in the realme, that weekelie collection shall be made for their helpe and sustentation, to the end they should not scatter abroad, and by begging here and there annoie both towne and countrie . . . But if they refuse to be supported by this benefit of law, and will rather indevor by going to and fro to mainteine their idle trades, then are they adjudged to be parcell of the third sort, and so in steed of courteous refreshing at home, are often corrected with sharp execution, and whip of justice abroad. (*Chronicles,* 1:307–8)

Harrison, who displays a fairly insightful understanding of other social issues, seems completely oblivious to the fact that many of these displaced poor had no community in which to reside, being driven from their homes by the very land practices that Harrison so soundly condemns in other parts of the "Description."

Other Abuses

Harrison does not limit his criticism only to rural issues but cites abuses at all levels of society. He complains of how at the universities, wealthy persons' bribes keep out poor scholars and gentlemen's sons receive fellowships that "were erected by their founders at the first, onelie for poor

mens sons, whose parents were not able to bring them up unto learning:
but now they have the least benefit of them, by reason the rich doo so
incroch upon them. And so farre hath this inconvenience spread it selfe,
that it is in my time an hard matter for a poor mans child to come by a
felowship (though he be never so good a scholer & woorthie of that
roome)" (*Chronicles*, 1:252). Harrison then notes that not only do the
rich keep poor and deserving students from the opportunity to study by
depriving them of the means to do so, but their sons waste these schol-
arships by spending their time gambling and with prostitutes rather
than studying. Harrison's complaint of the growing polarization
between rich and poor appears even at the university, where again the
wealthy unethically benefit at the poor's expense.

Harrison's pronouncements on the current state of England's legal
system are hardly more optimistic. As with the universities, he demonstrates how the powerful and wealthy exploit the courts to their advantage. In addition to the expected attack on the venality of lawyers, he
includes a scathing disclosure of a number of abuses in the jury system
itself, including how jurors are sometimes starved until they come up
with a verdict, and how common it is for "the craftier or stronger side to
procure and packe such a quest, as he himselfe shall like of, whereby he
is sure of the issue before the charge be given" (*Chronicles*, 1:262).

As an avid religious reformer, Harrison is also highly critical of the
contemporary church, which he views as only partially reformed and
still subject to a number of abuses, especially at the upper levels. Harrison's criticism of the upper clergy is a distinguishing characteristic of the
1587 "Description." He attacks clerical ambition and promotion and
cites historical example to reveal the bishops' desire for political power
by demonstrating how the various archbishops of Canterbury had
attempted to undermine the monarch's authority down through the
ages: "The archbishop of Canturburie is commonlie called primat of all
England; and in the coronations of the kings of this land, and all other
times, wherein it shall please the prince to weare and put on his crowne,
his office is to set it upon their heads. They beare also the name of their
high chapleins continuallie, although not a few of them have presumed
(in time past) to be their equals, and void of subjection to them" (*Chronicles*, 1:222). While Harrison applauds the removal of all images,
shrines, and stained-glass windows from the churches and the marked
reduction of religious festivals to only 27, he calls for even greater
reform in this area, stating that only Christmas, Easter, and Whitsun
should be observed and that all festivals of the Virgin Mary should be

abolished from the calendar "as neither necessarie nor commendable in a reformed church" (1:233).

Harrison's criticism of existing church practices also focuses on the plight of the lower clergy, and his many examples of their financial hardships come from his own experience, as he continually reminds the reader. Harrison describes how the lower clergy is forced to survive on meager benefices as well as bear the burden of excessive taxes imposed by both church and state:

> And to saie truth, one most commonlie of these small livings is of so little value, that it is not able to mainteine a meane scholar; much lesse a learned man, as not being above ten, twelve, sixteene, seventeene, twentie, or thirtie pounds at the most, toward their charges, which now (more than before time) doo go out of the same. I saie more than before, bicause everie small trifle, noble mans request, or courtesie craved by the bishop, dooth impose and command a twentith part, a three score part, or two pence in the pound, & c.: out of our livings, which hitherto hath not beene usuallie granted, but by consent of a synod, wherein things were decided according to equitie, and the poorer sort considered of, which now are equallie burdened. (*Chronicles,* 1:229)

Whether depicting church, town, or country, the portrait of England that Harrison offers in the 1587 "Description" shows a society divided into predator and prey. This portrait is developed through Harrison's relentless depiction of the methods used by the wealthy and powerful to exploit the poor and voiceless. Though the one constant of Harrison's social criticism is a pronounced class antagonism, he is not so completely careless as to present these views as his own. As Patterson has noted, when dealing with some of his more dangerous topics, such as the abuses practiced by the upper echelons of church and state, Harrison relies on a rhetorical device common to many radical sixteenth-century social critics: he displaces the commentary onto an unnamed source. Many of his more pointed critiques begin with such phrases as "some say," "this they say," "some wish," and even "but very many let not to saye," implying that even the mere thought is too dangerous for anyone to articulate, although this is exactly what he is doing (Patterson 1994, 63). Perhaps the most curious element of Harrison's social commentary is that in 1587 he was actually in a better position, both financially and professionally, than in 1577, having been made canon of Windsor in 1586. That Harrison's cynicism increased even when he was in a position of greater prosperity certainly argues for his disinterest in his own position when he decided to include such numerous criticisms in his revised "Description."

In Praise of England

Despite the significant amount of social criticism added to the 1587 "Description," Harrison does not completely abandon the optimistic view of all things English that characterize his earlier version of the text. The later "Description" still reveals touches of unabashed chauvinism, ranging from praise of English dogs to a detailed argument delineating the English right to sovereignty over the entire island of Britain, including Scotland. Most examples occur in the third book, which begins with seven chapters devoted to England's animals, both wild and domestic. Harrison continually reiterates the superiority of English animals in both quality and number: "For where are oxen commonlie more large of bone, horsses more decent and pleasant in passe, kine more commodious for the pale, sheepe more profitable for wooll, swine more wholesome of flesh, and goates more gainefull to their keepers than here with us in England?" (*Chronicles*, 1:369). He also boasts of the abundance of wild game, noting that "there is no nation under the sunne, which hath alreadie in the time of the yere more plentie of wild foule than we" (1:374). In describing "English dogs and their qualities," he offers his own mastiff as an example of their intelligence and faithfulness, describing how it refused entrance to anyone carrying a weapon and pulled from Harrison's hand the rod he used to discipline his children, "or else pluck downe their clothes to save them from the stripes" (1:388). Harrison's praise of anything native born extends even to his fellow Englishmen. His criticism of his countrymen's habits does not extend to their physical characteristics, as he notes them to be "of a good complexion, tall of stature, strong in bodie, white of colour, and thereto of great boldnesse and courage in the warres"(1:192–93).

Harrison's promotion of England's merits includes its native institutions as well as its natural resources. In a chapter devoted to celebrating the English navy, Harrison emphasizes the navy's importance in protecting England from foreign invasion, citing the historical precedents of the Romans, the Saxons, and the Danes, to prove how easily England could be invaded when it lacked coastal protection. His praise of England's navy appears prophetic when he states that "the common report that strangers make of our ships amongst themselves is dailie confirmed to be true, which is, that for strength, asurance, nimblenesse and swiftnesse of sailing, there are no vessels in the world to be compared with ours" (*Chronicles,* 1:337). In 1588, the English navy was to prove him correct. Harrison's singling out of the navy for praise has a deeper significance than the mere celebration of its reputed superiority. The purpose of the navy is to protect England from foreign invasion, to protect its integrity, its purity, its very "Englishness." In Harrison's view, foreign influences are always suspect. In his "Description," the navy becomes emblematic of England's ability to close off its borders and to maintain its identity as well as its security.

Harrison relies on history to substantiate English claims to political and religious purity as well. Integral to his vision of an England untainted by foreign influences is an England united under one crown. In chapter 23 of the first book, "After What Maner the Sovereigntie of this Ile dooth Remaine to the Princes of Lhogres or Kings of England," Harrison includes a brief history of Scottish and English relations to prove English sovereignty over Scotland and the English right to rule the entire island of Britain. Relying on the argument that Scotland had belonged to England since the time of Edward the Confessor and that English law had been observed in Scotland since that time, he lists the various Scottish kings who had sworn fealty to English sovereigns throughout the ages as further proof of his point. Although Harrison refrains from mentioning the obvious, his idealized vision of British unity would exclude Scotland's "Auld Alliance" with France, finally ridding the island of Britain of its one continual foreign presence.

In another example of English preeminence, Harrison bases his claim for the purity of the English church on the argument that the earliest inhabitants of Britain, supposedly descended from Noah, were monotheists who believed "that the soule of man is immortall, that God is omnipotent, mercifull as a father in shewing favor unto the godlie, and just as an upright judge in punishing the wicked; that the secrets of mans hart are not unknowne, and onelie knowne to him; and that as the world and all that is therein had their beginning by him, at his owne will, so shall all things likewise have an end, when he shall see his time" (*Chronicles,* 1:34). Harrison blamed the development of polytheism in ancient England on outside influences, pointing out that until the arrival of pagan interlopers from Egypt, "[I]t is not likelie that anie grosse idolatrie or superstition did enter in among us"(1:39).

The purpose of Harrison's detailed explanation of pre-Christian religious tradition soon becomes clear as he draws numerous parallels between "papist" and pagan practices, such as comparing the pagan deification of mortals and the ascribing of their names to certain celestial constellations to "the catalogue of Romish saints"(*Chronicles,* 1:39). Britain's pre-Christian religious purity corrupted by the pagan religious practices of invaders becomes the precedent for its early Christian purity corrupted by the heresy of Augustine of Canterbury. The Reformation is thus revealed as the final repurification of an English religious tradition that dates back not only to the country's first evangelization, but to its very origins. Harrison suggests, in another example of nativism, that as long as English religion remains independent of outside influences, it retains its true form, free of error and superstition. Whether discussing dogs, the navy, or religion, Harrison's English chauvinism is consistent; the key to England's well-being depends on the maintenance of English integrity through its isolation from foreign customs.

Harrison's Accomplishment

It appears from various comments and material in the "Description of England" that Harrison conceived of his work as not only a description, but also as a manual full of useful information. He originally had envisioned a section on the ports and creeks of England as extensive as his section on rivers, which alone account for six of the first book's 24 chapters. Unfortunately, Harrison tells us, "[I]t came to passe that the greater part of my labor was taken from me by stealth," and the extensive section "whose knowledge I am right sure would have been profitable: and for the which I hoped to have reaped great thankes at the hands of such sea-faring men, as whould have had use hereof," remained a short chapter (*Chronicles,* 1:181–82).

Harrison was able to include detailed instructions for those skills he or others of his household possessed, such as the planting and harvesting of saffron, the brewing of beer, the preparation of brawn, and the cultivation of medicinal herbs. He devotes an entire chapter to saffron, including a detailed description of the crocus, its cultivation, the medicinal properties of saffron, and the profit that could be realized from saffron production. He justifies the inclusion of the chapter by pointing to its "usefulness": "Would to God that my countriemen had beene heretofore (or were now) more carefull of this commoditie! then would it no doubt have prooved more beneficiall to our Iland than our cloth or wooll" (*Chronicles,* 1:391). Besides explanations of how to perform various tasks, Harrison also offers his readers warnings of unethical business practices, such as the underhanded dealings of local merchants, the manner in which inn hostellers cheated horses of their food, and the ease with which unwary travelers could be robbed by inn employees (1:415). This information is of a cautionary as well as useful nature and appears to have been designed not only to warn consumers but also to reveal to the authorities the extent of such abuses. The third book's lists of the dates and locations of country fairs and markets as well as the number of miles between major cities and towns also appear to have been included for their benefit to Harrison's readers.

In spite of Harrison's scholarly and utilitarian intentions, the "Description" at times becomes a highly personal manifesto, especially in those sections where he relies on oral tradition and personal knowledge. His social critiques range from sensitive and compassionate portrayals of the sufferings of the rural poor to fits of pique over perceived slights, such as when in describing the various towns along the Linus River, he sourly notes that one of them "at one time might have beene my living if I would have given sir Thomas Rugband money inough, but now it belongeth to Gundevill and Caius college in Cambridge" (*Chronicles,* 1:175).

The markedly personal nature of the "Description" is underscored by Harrison's employment of the first-person narrative voice throughout much of the text, particularly in those sections where he speaks from his own experience. At times this leads to confusion, as when he continues to use the first person in presenting information from other sources. Though he clearly states in his "Epistle Dedicatorie" that he has never traveled, he employs the first person in describing the various islands and rivers of chapters 10 through 16 in the first book. Such statements as "We left the rocke on our left hand, and came straight southwest to Helford haven," or "Being passed the Loo, I came to another water that descendeth without anie increase from Crowan by Simneie" strike the reader as odd, given Harrison's admission earlier that he has visited none of these locations. The confusion clears when one consults Leland and realizes that these passages are lifted almost directly from Leland's notes, which are also written in the first person. Why Harrison would adopt the first-person narrative voice here is difficult to understand, especially since it results in such bizarre sentence constructions as "Leaving this water we sailed on, casting about the Nash point, omitting two or three small waters (whereof Leland hath alreiade as ye see made mention) because I have nothing more to add unto their descriptions, except it be, that the Colhow taketh in a rill from Lan Iltruit, of whose course (to saie the truth) I have no manner of knowledge" (*Chronicles,* 1:129).

Harrison switches his voice from that of a first-person eyewitness to that of someone citing another's information because he has no knowledge of what he has just described. He may have been trying to make the description more vivid and immediate for the reader. He may have felt it necessary to quote Leland verbatim, as he states at various points, "And hitherto Leland, whose words I dare not alter," although his claims of remaining faithful to Leland's words are contradicted by his paraphrasing of Leland in other parts of the text (1:118).

Harrison's style is rambling, digressive, and chatty. He appears fully conscious of his tendency to wander, calling himself and the reader back to the topic at hand with such phrases as "But whither have I slipped?" (*Chronicles*, 1:281) or "But whither am I digressed?" (1:400), or "But how farre am I gone from my purpose?" (1:115). Many of his tangents begin with specific references to England and continue with elaborate examples of similar occurrences in other periods and other climates. For example, he describes the Ile of Burhoo as the "Ile of rats, so called of the huge plentie of rats that are found there." Harrison then lists various other places in which vermin drove out the human population, providing 12 examples in all, many from classical sources such as Varro and Pliny (1:57). At other times he goes off on tangents that have even less to do with his topic, as when a chapter entitled "What sundrie nations have dwelled in Albion" becomes entirely devoted to the question of the existence of giants.

Although Harrison has a keen appreciation for tales of the bizarre, he approaches local superstitions and folk beliefs with great suspicion and makes no effort to hide his disdain for those who give them credence. For example, in his description of English meadows, he notes a charm employed to protect cattle from disease:

> some superstitious fooles suppose that they which die of the garget are ridden with the night mare, and therefore they hang up stones which naturallie have holes in them, and must be found unlooked for: as if such a stone were an apt cockeshot for the divell to run through and solace himselfe withall, whilest the cattell go scot free and are not molested by him. But if I should set downe but halfe the toies that superstition hath brought into our husbandmens heads in this and other behalfes, it would aske a greater volume than is convenient for such a purpose, wherefore it shall suffice to have said thus much of these things. (*Chronicles*, 1:183)

Harrison dismisses anything that he felt could not be proven by scientific, classical, or scriptural sources. Furthermore, his reformist tendencies lead him to a general condemnation of folk festivals and celebrations. His attitude toward native folk belief and tradition tends to be highly disparaging, and for this reason the "Description," despite its vast size and thoroughness in every other area, is not a particularly good resource for English folklore.

Harrison's skepticism is further manifested in his chapter on the "Marvels of England." He specifically refuses to include supernatural marvels, a point that he stresses with his opening observation, "Such that have written of the woonders of our countrie in old time, have spoken (no doubt) of manie things which deserve no credit at all" (*Chronicles,* 1:217). As an example, he offers a story from Gervaise of Tilbury about a ghostly knight that challenged visitors who wandered into his haunt in Wandleburie hills, concluding with the remark, "But let who so list beleeve it, sith it is either a fable devised, or some divelish illusion, if anie such thing were doone." Harrison then declares that he will provide tales of wonders "either I know my selfe to be true, or am crediblie informed to be so" (1:217). Harrison's distrust of any claims to the existence of supernatural phenomena distinguishes him from the other contributors to Holinshed's *Chronicles,* who often appear more willing to believe in monstrous beasts, ghosts, or other prodigious portents.

The marvels that Harrison includes in the "Description" are strikingly different from the ones found in the rest of the *Chronicles* in that they consist only of natural and provable phenomena. Of Stonehenge, he admits that he has no definite explanation for its appearance but that he suspects the ancient Britons built it as a burial memorial for those slaughtered by the Saxons. Other wonders that he lists include the Chedderhole in Somerset shire, "whereinto manie men have entred & walked verie farre. Howbeit, as the passage is large and nothing noisome: so diverse that have adventured to go into the same, could never as yet find the end of that waie, neither see anie other thing than pretie riverets and streames"; a stone "not farre from saint Davids, which is verie great, as a bed, or such like thing: and being raised up, a man may stirre it with his thumbe; but not with his shoulder or force of his whole bodie"; and a well in "Darbieshire called Tideswell . . . whose water often seemeth to rise and fall, as the sea which is fortie miles from it dooth usualle accustome to ebb and flow. And hereof an opinion is groweth that it keepeth an ordinarie course as the sea dooth" (*Chronicles,* 1:217–20). Harrison's decision to include only those marvels that he considers worthy of mention and his articulation of that choice underscore the highly idiosyncratic nature of most of the "Description." In many ways "The Description of England" that appears in Holinshed's *Chronicles* is not simply *a* description of England, but a description of *Harrison's* England, shaped by the time and place in which he lived. No other example of the genre displays such a uniquely personal point of view.

The interest of "The Description of England" lies not only in its detailed portrayal of English life in the sixteenth century but also in its articulation of the concerns of an average English citizen responding to the dizzying economic and social transformations taking place around him. Highly opinionated and skeptical of the official discourse of the time, Harrison reveals a profound understanding of how the growing emphasis on individual success and wealth and the increased urbanization of England's population was contributing to the disintegration of those ties of hospitality, charity, and duty that held rural communities together. While he often complains of situations that affect him personally, he is extremely sensitive to the plight of the rural poor, which is not surprising given his position as a country pastor. Although working within the established literary tradition of the historical description, Harrison created a document that far outshines its antecedents in its detail, thoroughness, and immediacy, giving us not only a description of the country but an intimate portrait of the man.

Chapter Four
The "Chronicles of Ireland"

Although we think of Holinshed's *Chronicles* primarily as a source of information for English cultural and national history, it is also a valuable document of Irish history and culture, particularly the period under Tudor rule. The Irish section of Holinshed's *Chronicles* offers us a fascinating insight into Irish cultural identity and English colonialism during the Elizabethan era, primarily because two of the major contributors to the 1577 and 1587 editions, Richard Stanyhurst and John Hooker, were personally involved in these issues. Whereas Raphael Holinshed contributed the first two books of the Irish history, Richard Stanyhurst, the scion of a prominent Anglo-Irish family, wrote the "Description of Ireland" and "Thirde Booke of the Historie of Ireland" for the 1577 *Chronicles,* and John Hooker, an English colonizer, provided a translation of Giraldus Cambrensis's *Expugnatio Hibernica* (*Conquest of Ireland*) and the "Supplie of the Irish Chronicles," an update of the Irish history from Edward VI's reign to 1586, for the 1587 publication.

The 1577 edition of the *Chronicles* draws heavily on Edmund Campion's *Historie of Ireland* (1571).[1] Campion, as he relates in the dedication to his patron, the Earl of Leicester, wrote his history in 10 short weeks during the end of his sojourn in Ireland, using the manuscripts and personal recollections of his host, James Stanyhurst, an influential member of the Anglo-Irish community. Although he had been ordained an Anglican deacon in 1568, Campion was still suspected of papist leanings and was in hiding when he wrote the history in 1571. Campion's work, gathered out of Anglo-Irish sources, was revised and expanded by Raphael Holinshed for the first two books of the 1577 "Historie of Ireland" and by Richard Stanyhurst, James's son and Campion's student and friend, for inclusion in "The Thirde Booke of the Historie of Ireland" and the 1577 "Description of Ireland." The final product reflects the point of view of the Anglo-Irish community that saw Ireland as its home but not its culture, mediated through the writings of an English Catholic, which in turn were expanded and edited by an English Protestant.

The "Description of Ireland"

Dedicated to Sir Henry Sidney, lord deputy of Ireland from 1565 to 1571, Richard Stanyhurst's "Description of Ireland" is both a portrait and a defense of his native land. Divided into eight chapters of varying length, the first half of the "Description" lays out the geographical resources of Ireland, both natural and human. The second half focuses on Ireland's two populations, the Gaelic and the Anglo. The purpose of the "Description," as Stanyhurst states in his dedication to Sidney, is "to the better understanding of the histories," that is, to provide a geographical and anthropological context for Ireland's tumultuous past (*Irish*, 7). Stanyhurst's deep love of his country and pride in his own Anglo-Irish community manifests itself throughout the text as he painstakingly depicts the numerous natural beauties of Ireland and the various accomplishments of the Anglo Irish, but his colonist's mistrust of the Gaelic Irish results in a dismissive, sketchy, and ultimately unsatisfactory portrait of Ireland's native population. Nevertheless, Stanyhurst's fervent belief that the Gaelic Irish were ultimately reformable, and that their behavior and manners stemmed from ignorance rather than intrinsic vice, was a far more conciliatory view of the Gaels than that of most contemporary English commentators on Ireland, who tended to depict them as unregenerate beasts.

Despite his reputation as one of the worst poets to come out of the English Renaissance, Stanyhurst is an engaging and amusing prose narrator and an excellent storyteller. His delight in coining words and phrases, love of alliteration, and extensive use of colloquial language add an interesting liveliness to his writings. He refers to the lazy as "idle benchewhistlers" and "luskishe faytoures" (*Irish*, 52). Any critic of his stance toward the Irish language is "some snappish carper [who] will . . . snuffingly snibbe me, for debacing the Irish language." He warns against "beating Jack for Jyll," in his depiction of the English Pale's various problems (15). Stanyhurst's contributions to the Irish section are some of the most entertaining and readable in the entire *Chronicles* and a welcome relief from Holinshed's fragmented and cursory Irish history or Hooker's plodding "Supplie."

Stanyhurst begins the "Description" with a discussion of the various etymologies of Ireland's name; a brief sketch of the country's main provinces of Leinster, Connaught, Ulster, Munster, and Meath and of those provinces' shires and counties; and then an account of the division

of Ireland into the English Pale and the Irishry. His depiction of the differences between the Anglo-Irish community of the Pale and the Gaelic
Irish serves as starting point for a detailed discussion of the role of language and culture in the conquest of Ireland. In Stanyhurst's view, the
major obstacles to the complete colonization of Ireland were Irish language, dress, and custom. He believed that to remove these from the
Gaelic Irish and supply in their stead English language, dress, and tradition would easily solve England's continuing problems with Ireland. Of
course, the reality of the situation was that cultural transformation usually passed in the opposite direction, with the Anglo Irish, particularly
those beyond the Pale, taking on Gaelic-Irish ways. For this reason,
Stanyhurst was a great proponent of a program of education and reform
to "improve" the condition of those who lived beyond the Pale, and he
expressed continual anxiety over the infusion of native Irish language
and culture into the Pale.

Certainly Stanyhurst's biggest concern seems to be the Anglo-Irish
propensity to "go native," and his "Description" is filled with dire warning of what happened when the English took on the customs, language,
and dress of the native Irish: "For as my skill is very simple therein, so I
woulde be loth to disveyle my rashnesse, in giving light verdict in anything to me unknown: but onely my short discourse tendeth to this
drift, that it is not expedient that the Irishe tongue should be so univer-
sally gagled in the English pale: bycause that by proofe and experience
we see, that the pale was never in more florishing estate than when it
was wholly English, & never in woorse plight then since it hath en-
fraunchysed the Irishe (*Irish,* 15).

According to Stanyhurst, the most fearsome example of English
decline appeared in Ulster, which over the centuries had reverted back
to an almost wholly Gaelic enclave:

> It is knowen, and by the hystorie you maye in part perceyve, how bravely
> Ulster whillon floorished. The Englishe families were there implanted,
> the Irish eyther utterly expelled or wholly subdued, the lawes duely exe-
> cuted, the revenue great, and onely English spoken. But what brought it
> to this present ruine and decay? I doubt not, but you gesse, before I tell
> you. They were environned and compassed with evill neighbours. Neigh-
> bourhood bredde acquaintance, acquaintance wafted in the Irish tongue,
> the Irishe hooked with it attyre, attyre haled rudenes, rudenesse engen-
> dred ignorance, ignoraunce brought contempt of lawes, the contempt of
> lawes bred rebellion, rebellion raked thereto warres, and so consequently
> the utter decay and desolation of that worthy countrey. (*Irish,* 16)

Time and time again, Stanyhurst describes the Irish culture as a kind of disease or corrupting infection against which one must constantly guard. The Irish language is a "tettar" or "ringworm" that harbors itself "within the jaws of English conquerers." He warns that when "the Irish language was free dennized in the English pale: this canker tooke such deep roote, as the body that before was whole and sounde, was by little and little festered, and in maner wholy putrified" (*Irish*, 14).

The fear of "going native" and of its accompanying degenerative symptoms were not merely idiosyncratic obsessions of Stanyhurst's as articulated in the "Description of Ireland" but a continuing concern of the English Crown. In 1306, the Crown proclaimed the Statutes of Kilkenny, which remained in effect until the seventeenth century. The statutes forbade, under harsh penalty, the English to speak Irish or to wear Irish dress or hairstyles. It also outlawed Irish music, poetry, and games and severely limited foreign commerce. Intermarriage with the Irish and the fostering of Anglo-Norman children in Irish families was defined as high treason.[2] It appears that these draconian measures were not enforced with particular enthusiasm, since the Anglo Irish beyond the Pale continued to assimilate into the native Irish community for more than two hundred fifty years.

After his ominous warnings against permitting Irish language and customs in the Pale, Stanyhurst turns to a pseudoscientific analysis of the language itself, citing Giraldus Cambrensis's claim that Irish is a composite of every existing known tongue, including Scythyian, Egyptian, Greek, Danish, and Spanish. Stanyhurst admits that he has little knowledge of Irish, but this does not stop him from commenting extensively on it. To illustrate the difficulty of the language, which he claims "scarce one in five hundred can eyther reader, wryte, or understande" and "very fewe in the country can attayne to the perfection thereof, and much lese a forreinner or estraunger," Stanyhurst includes an anecdote, typical of the many that grace his text: "A gentleman of mine acquaintance reported that he dyd see a woman in Rome, which was possest with a babbling spirite, that coulde have chatted any language saving the Irishe, and that it was so difficult as the very Devyll was graveyled therewith." When one gentleman present protested that it was because the language was "too sacred and holy" to be uttered by demons, another cleverly retorted, "I stande in doubt, I tell you, whether the apostles in theyr copious marte of languages at Jerusalem coulde have spoken Irishe, if they were opposed" (*Irish*, 18). Stanyhurst concludes his discussion of the Irish language with a number of rambling digressions,

such as the lack of an Irish word for "knave," a peculiarity that he claims
it shares with Greek, and the etymology of "pogh," a contemptuous
term used by the Anglo Irish for the Gaelic Irish, which, according to
Stanyhurst, evolved from the dismissive Irish interjection "boagh."

After providing a brief description of Ireland's low and watery soil,
wholesome air, and temperate climate, Stanyhurst turns to one of Ireland's most notable attributes, its lack of snakes and other poisonous
creatures. Claiming that "no venomous creeping beast is brought forth,
or nourished, or can live in Ireland, being brought or sent," he provides
a series of anecdotes to support his statement, including the tale of a
young Englishman who, suffering internally from the gnawing of a
snake that he had swallowed while sleeping, traveled to Ireland and
"dyd not sooner drinke of the water of that Islande, and taken of the
victuals of Ireland, but forthwith he kilde the Snake, avoyed it
downewarde, and so being lustye and lively he returned into Englande."
After quoting a number of authorities as to whether Saint Patrick's
expulsion of all snakes out of Ireland or the nature of the soil itself is
responsible for this phenomenon, Stanyhurst ingenuously concludes the
discussion by noting that he himself holds no opinion on the matter
(*Irish,* 22). The chapter concludes with a rather haphazard account of
Ireland's flora and fauna in which Stanyhurst lists the country's various
wild and domestic beasts as well as both cultivated and native vegeta-
tion.

Stanyhurst's affection for Ireland most thoroughly manifests itself in
his next topic, his native Dublin, which he affectionately describes as
"the beautie and eye of Ireland." Through a number of anecdotes, he
develops a historical description of Dublin, focusing particularly on the
legendary hospitality of Dublin's mayors. It soon becomes apparent that
the mayors' hospitality is emblematic of Dublin's prosperity and bounty
as a whole, for "not onely their officers so farre excell in hospitalite, but
also the greater parte of the civitie is generally addicted to such ordinarie and standing houses, as it woulde make a man muse which way
they are able to beare it out, but onely by the goodnesse of God which is
the Upholder and Furtherer of hospitalitie" (*Irish,* 42). A detailed
account of the various churches of Dublin as well as its streets, bridges,
lanes, and other notable places concludes Stanyhurst's depiction of his
beloved city. Stanyhurst continues his chapter on Ireland's cities and
towns with descriptions of Waterford, Limerick, Cork, Drogheda, Ross,
Weisford, Kilkenny, and Thomastowne. His love of anecdote reveals
itself in his inclusion of various local folklore and histories, including the

lively tales of Rose, admired benefactress of Ross, and the abbot Kanicus, namesake of the town of Kilkenny. The chapter closes with a discussion of the mythical origins of Ireland's five provinces and the regions into which each of the provinces were divided.

In his fourth chapter, Stanyhurst turns to the "estraunge and wonderfull places in Irelande." His narrative draws heavily from Campion's *Historie,* which in turn employs Giraldus Cambrensis's *Topographia.* Giraldus's fascination with the bizarre and the fantastic, as well as his credulity concerning such matters, drew the derision of Renaissance historians, and Stanyhurst makes every effort to protect himself from any accusations of the same gullibility. Stanyhurst often articulates his skepticism, noting where he has personally investigated the existence of the various marvels since he would not "wish any to be so light as to lende his credite to any such fayned gloses as are neyther veryfied by experience nor warranted by any coulourable reason" (*Irish,* 67). Despite his protestations, he does not hesitate to include a detailed catalog of Ireland's fabled prodigies, including the country's numerous miraculous lakes, streams, and wells. In Munster, he notes the existence of a well that turns hair washed in its water to gray, , and in Ulster a well whose water turns gray hair back to its original color. He cites the existence of a lake, also in Ulster, created by a woman who forgot to put the lid on a holy well; consequently, the water from the well flooded the entire countryside. Stanyhurst devotes considerable space to St. Patrick's Purgatory, a pilgrimage site where the faithful enter to see visions of hell, but Stanyhurst, following Campion, dismisses the visions that pilgrims over the centuries claimed to have experienced. Stanyhurst notes that he had spoken to a number of pilgrims himself whose only visions were "fearful dreams when they chanced to nod" (67).

In concluding his chapter Stanyhurst turns with a touch of irony to Ireland's true natural marvels—its rich mineral stores: "Such notable quarries of grey marble and touch, such store of pearle & other riche stones, such aboundaunce of cole, such plentie of leade, yron, latten [a mineral similar to brass] and tinne, so many rich mynes furnished with all kinde of metals, as nature seemed to have framed this countrey for the storehouse or jewelhouse of hir chiefest thesaure [treasure]." Unfortunately, native apathy has left these treasures untouched, and Stanyhurst notes that although nature, instead of being "so bountifull a mother in powring foorth such riches," has proven an "envious stepdame" in that she "instilleth in the inhabitants a drousie lythernesse to withdraw them from the ensearching of hir hourded and hidden jewelles." Stanyhurst goes on to compare the situation to that of inviting "divers guestes to costly and daintie dinner," but through enchantment depriving them of the use of their limbs or of their appetite so that they are unable "by taking theyr repast, to refresh themselves" (*Irish,* 72–73). The inhabitants to whom Stanyhurst refers appear to be the Gaelic Irish rather than his own Anglo-Irish community, whose industry, resourcefulness, and hard work he celebrates throughout the "Description." As such, the passage can also be read as a defense of the colonial endeavor, since it is the Anglo Irish rather than the native Gaels who possess the qualities necessary to appreciate the true marvels of Ireland.

Chapters 5 through 8, which list and describe the various communities and notable personalities of Ireland, reveal Stanyhurst's strong identification with the Anglo Irish of the Pale. As a response to English perceptions of Ireland as backward and ignorant, he carefully highlights the many intellectual achievements of primarily the Anglo Irish, but also the Gaelic Irish, in the fields of law, philosophy, religion, and letters, devoting the entirety of chapter 5 to the bishops and archbishops of Ireland and chapter 7 to "the learned men and authours of Ireland."

The Anglo-Irish assimilation that Stanyhurst disparaged in his discussion of the Irish language again appears as an issue in the sixth chapter, "The lordes temporall, as well English as Irishe, which inhabite Ireland," where the list of the ancient nobility includes the names of Anglo-Irish barons who assimilated completely into Gaelic-Irish culture, some even leading revolts against the English Crown. Though most of the chapter is devoted to the history of Stanyhurst's employers, the Kildare branch of the Fitzgeralds, it also refers to a number of nobles, who, except for their ancestry, were essentially Gaelic-Irish in custom and language: "Lord Bermingham, baron of Athenrie, nowe degenerate and become meere Irish, against whome hys auncestors served valiauntly in the yere 1300"; "L. Courcy, not verie Irishe; the auncient descent of the Courcies planted in Ireland wyth the conquest"; "Mack Surtan, L. Desert, hys auncestours were Lordes in the tyme of Lionel, Duke of Clarence, Erle of Ulster, in the yeare 1360, now very wyld Irish"; "Den, Banret of Pormanstown, waxing Irish" (reinforcing Stanyhurst's metaphor of Irish culture and language as a degenerative disease); and among those "English gentlemen of longest continuance in Ireland" is "fitz Ursulies, now degenerate, and called in Irish, Mack Mahon, the Beares sonne" (*Irish,* 88–95). Although Stanyhurst does not openly acknowledge the fact, his list reveals that the Anglo-Irish community itself was divided between those who maintained a strong allegiance to the Crown, primarily the Pale inhabitants, and those who strove to establish political autonomy.

As noted earlier, Stanyhurst takes great pains in his "Description" to delineate the differences between his own Anglo-Irish community and the "meere" or native Gaelic Irish. In his last chapter, "The disposition and maners of the meere Irish, commonly called the wyld Irishe," he stresses to the reader the difference between the Gaelic Irish whom he is about to describe and the Anglo Irish of the Pale: "Before I attempt the unfolding of the maners of the meere Irish, I thinke it expedient, to fore-warne thee, reader, not to impute anie barbarous custome that shall be here laid downe, to the citizens, townesmen, and inhabitants of the English pale, in that they differ little or nothyng from the auncient cus-tomes and dispositions of their progenitors, the English and Walshmen, beyng therefore as mortallie behated of the Irish, as those who are borne in England" (*Irish,* 112). In this passage, Stanyhurst underscores the identification between the Anglo Irish and the English by pointing out that the Gaelic Irish make no distinctions between the two, although during Elizabeth's reign, a sense of separate national identity had actu-ally intensified among the Anglo Irish, especially those who lived beyond the Pale. This resulted in part from their increasing alienation from the newly arrived English who, as a result of Elizabethan Irish pol-icy, appropriated the administrative positions traditionally held by the Anglo Irish and, in a number of cases, their property and landholdings as well. If, as Stanyhurst claims, the Gaelic Irish saw the Anglo Irish and the English as the same community, neither the Anglo Irish nor the newly arrived English saw themselves as such.

Stanyhurst's description of the Gaelic Irish is a haphazard listing of physical traits, diet, dress, schooling practices, legal system, customs, and religious superstitions, such as leaving the right arm of their chil-dren unchristened so that it might give "a more ungracious and deadly blowe." Though he clearly views the Gaelic Irish as inferior to his own community, he does not hesitate to acknowledge their virtues and their strengths, continually emphasizing the role of education as a civilizing influence: "religious, franke, amorous, ireful, sufferable of infinite paynes, very glorious, many sorcerers, excellent horsemen, delighted with wars, great almesgivers, passing in hospitality. The lewder sort, both clearkes and lay men, are sensuall & over loose in livying. The same, beying ver-tuously bred up or reformed, are such myrrors of holynes and austeritie that other nations retaine but a shadow of devotion in comparison of them" (*Irish,* 112–13).

The last chapter of the "Description of Ireland" clearly demonstrates that although Stanyhurst regards the Gaelic-Irish leaders with suspicion, demonstrates disdain for the customs and beliefs of the Gaelic-Irish community, and continually emphasizes the differences between that community and his own, he believes that the Gaelic Irish are redeemable and that through a program of education and legal reform, they could easily be civilized and "uplifted." Despite his superior stance, his attitude toward the Gaelic Irish is far more charitable and even inclusive than that of other contemporary English commentators on Ireland, who for the most part advocated violent force to subdue the Gaels. Throughout the "Description," Stanyhurst articulates his belief that Gaelic-Irish "weaknesses" are due to custom, not breeding. He ends the "Description" with a prayer demonstrating his argument that through proper training and example, the Gaels could be successfully incorporated into the commonwealth:

> God with the beames of hys grace, clarifie the eyes of that rude people, that at length they may see theyr miserable estate: and also that such as are deputed to the governement therof bend their industry with conscionable pollicye to reduce them from rudenesse to knowledge, from rebellion to obedience, from trechery to honesty, from savagenesse to civilitie, from idlenes to labour, from wickednesse to godlynesse, whereby they may the sooner ... frame themselves plyable to the lawes and ordinaunces of hir majestie, whom God with his gracious assistance preserve, as to the happye reformation of hir realme of Ireland. (*Irish,* 116)

Stanyhurst, with a true reformer's zeal, sincerely believed that the widespread establishment of English law and custom was the answer to Ireland's problems and would result in a united, prosperous, and peaceful country; the events of the succeeding years were to prove him wrong.

The 1577 "Historie of Ireland"

The 1577 "Historie of Ireland" is divided into three books: the first relates the early history of Ireland from its first settlement to the Anglo-Norman invasion, the second traces the country's history from the reign of Henry II (1167) through the reign of Henry VII (1509), and the third presents those events that took place during the reign of Henry VIII (1509–1547). The same generalized woodcuts that appear in the 1577 English and Scottish histories are used to illustrate various Irish political events as well, although one woodcut, that of a primitive war band fleeing a slightly more civilized-looking group of warriors, is unique to the Irish history (*Irish*, xviii, 120). The Irish history lacks the formulaic woodcuts of various kings situated at the beginning of each monarch's reign that appear in the English and Scottish histories. Because of the absence of this ordering device, the chronology of the Irish history is not as clearly apparent to the reader.

While Holinshed has never been noted for his rhetorical sophistication or grace, the style of the Irish history is even more awkward and hurried than that of his other contributions to the *Chronicles*. As Anne Castanien has noted, "[H]is work here resembles rough jottings for an outline, without organization detail, and interpretation" (Castanien, 101). Any commentary that Holinshed provides is cursory, usually displaying skepticism about his sources, especially when they contradict claims of English sovereignty in Ireland or when they present religious material contradictory to English Protestantism.

In his dedication to Sir Henry Sidney, Holinshed relates how he incorporated Campion's work into his sections of the Irish history and how Richard Stanyhurst came to be involved in the writing of the final book of the history:

> I resolved to make shift to frame a speciall Historie of Irelande, in like maner as I had done of other Regions, followyng Campions order, and setting downe his owne wordes, excepte in places where I had mater to inlarge that (out of other Authours) which he had written in briefe: and this have I thought good to signifie, the rather for that I esteeme it good dealing in no wise to defraude him of his due deserved prayse. But now after I had continued the Historie, and enlarged it out of Giraldus Cambrensis, Flatsbury, Henry of Marleburgh, and other, till the yeare 1509, in which that famous prince Henry viii began his reigne; of those that were to bestow the charges of the Impression, procured a learned Gentleman Maister Richard Stanyhurst, to continue it from thenceforwarde as he was occasion, being furnished with mater to enlarge the worke, thereof for those latter time I founde my selfe utterly voyde, more than that whiche Campion had delivered. (*Irish*, 3 – 4)

The dedication reveals Holinshed's methodology in constructing the "Historie of Irelande" as well as his frustration with his lack of resources, a common complaint throughout the *Chronicles*. Indeed, Campion's text, which covers the course of Irish history from Noah to Henry VIII, is little more than a pamphlet. In the "Preface to the Reader," which immediately follows his dedication to the "Chronicles of England," Holinshed again voices an awareness of the problematic nature of the Irish history that goes beyond the traditional modesty motif found in Renaissance prefatory comments. The passage reveals a genuine frustration with the conditions under which he labored to produce his work and a dissatisfaction with the final result: "For Ireland, I have shewed in mine epistle dedicatorie in what sort, and by what helps I have proceeded therein; onlie this I forgot to signifie, that I had not Giraldus Cambrensis, and Flatsburie, untill that parte of the booke was under the presse, and so being constreined to make poste haste, I could not exemplifie what I would out of them all, neither yet dispose it so orderlie as had beene convenient, nor pen it with so apt words as might satisfie either myselfe, or those to whose view it is now like to come" (*Chronicles,* 2:vii). These same sentiments are again articulated at the end of the Irish history's second book, where Holinshed laments the haste with which he was forced to compile his Irish text. Nevertheless, despite his lack of time and his disorganization in assembling the first two books of the Irish history, Holinshed was able to construct a clearly focused theme that forms the ordering principle of his text: the historical inability of the Irish to govern themselves without descending into intestine squabbles, and the legitimacy of England's claim to Ireland.

The first book justifies Henry II's later invasion of Ireland by establishing an early precedent for England's sovereignty over the island and by denigrating other nations' claims to Ireland, specifically those of Scotland. As is typical in medieval and early Renaissance historical chronicles, its depiction of the ancient history of Ireland is filled with fictional claims and implausible legends, drawn primarily from Campion's borrowings from Giraldus Cambrensis. Although Holinshed includes these fantastical and often conflicting reports, he dismisses their veracity, inviting his readers to make their own evaluation of the material:

Although undoubtedlye, the originall of all nations for the more part is so uncertaine that who so ever shall enter into the searche thereof further than hee fyndeth in the holie scriptures, may seeme (as it were) rather to talk with men that dreame than to gather authorities sufficient whereupon to grounde any warranted opinion: yet for as muche as the authors (whom in this Irish hystorie we chiefly followe) have set downe what they have founde in the Irishe antiquities, concerning the firste inhabitation of this countrey of Ireland: and bycause the reader also maye be peradventure desirous to understande the same, we have thoughte good to recite what they have written thereof, leavying the credite unto the due consid-

eration of the circumspecte reader and, where the errours are too grosse,
giving by the waye some cautions, in lyke sorte as oure Authours themselves have done. (*Irish*, 117)

Holinshed supplies information with the assumption that his readers
will have the discernment to decide which sources can be believed and
which cannot, yet he does not leave them completely to their own
devices, for he provides critical guideposts in the form of marginal notes
or intertextual comments to aid their evaluation. For example, when he
relates Ireland's claim to having first been settled by the niece of the Old
Testament patriarch Noah, he points out the improbability of such an
origin, since "the Arte of sayling was unknowne to the world before the
universall floud"(*Irish*, 118). He concedes that Ireland was discovered
and populated by other of Noah's descendants three hundred years after
the Flood as well as by giants who were descended from Nimrod, then
continues his narrative with a series of subsequent invasions by the
Greeks, Scythians, Britons, and Spaniards. He devotes a considerable
amount of space to the Spanish settlement of Ireland, because, in his
opinion, this is the most believable story of origin "as both their own
histories and the Britishe do wholly agree." More importantly, the
Spaniards' settlement of Ireland also supports ancient claims of English
sovereignty over Ireland. According to the legends, Gurguntius, king of
the Britons, gave Ireland to the Spaniards to settle, since at that time
"he held the Irishe in subjection" with great difficulty. From this story
and from the dubious claims of Geoffrey of Monmouth, Holinshed
draws the triumphant conclusion that "the kings of thys our Britayn
had an elder right to the realme of Ireland than by the conquest of
Henry the seconde, whiche title they ever mainteyned, and somtimes
prevayled in pursuing therof, as in the dayes of king Arthure, to whome
the Irish (as in some histories is remembred) acknowledged their due
subjection"(125).

The origin of the five ancient kingdoms of Ireland, Leinster, Connaught, Ulster, Munster, and Meath, and of the traditional primacy of
one king over the other four forms the next part of the narrative, which
then turns to the intertwined histories of Ireland and Scotland, including the arrival of the shipwrecked Picts in Ireland (after a long journey
from Scythia); the intermarriage of the Irish and the Picts; and the
arrival of the Irish in northern Britain, resulting in the formation of
Scotland. Holinshed concludes the section on the interrelationship of the
ancient Irish and the Scots with a rebuttal to the Scottish claims of sov-

ereignty in Ireland. According to Scottish tradition, King Gregory, who reigned about 875, pretending title to Ireland by lawful succession, invaded and conquered the country: "And therefore some of the Scottes woulde seeme to make the conquest of Henry the seconde in Irelande a revoltyng from the righte inheritours, although they confesse they can not tell howe they came from the possession of it otherwyse than by forging a tale that they willingly forewent it" (*Irish,* 132). Although Holinshed includes the Scottish point of view in his history, his manner of framing this information within the narrative clearly points to his rejection of its truth.

After his treatment of ancient Irish and Scottish relations, Holinshed turns to the Christianization of Ireland and to the lives of the Irish saints. As usual, he incorporates various and conflicting reports of these events, including the claim that Ireland was partially evangelized by Saint James the Apostle, the Scottish account that a Pictish serving woman brought Christianity to Ireland through her conversion of the Irish queen, and finally the commonly held belief that Saint Patrick converted the island.

An example of the interplay of voices and views that characterize the *Chronicles* appears in this section on the Irish saints, which like much of the Irish history is borrowed almost verbatim from Campion's *Historie of Ireland.* Despite the fact that Campion, as a Catholic, shared the same religious beliefs as the Gaelic Irish, he displays no sense of identification with and little sympathy for them. He writes of the Irish, both Anglo and Gaelic, with a bemused and superior distance, satirizing both customs and beliefs. However, we see a striking change in tone as he turns his attention to the Irish saints, whose histories he treats with serious consideration. Holinshed, as is his usual editorial practice, lets Campion's text speak for itself, but as a Protestant divine, he faces the dilemma of including an obviously Catholic depiction of some fairly dubious saints' lives. Ever the diplomat, he inserts at the conclusion of this section a caveat that does not exactly negate the saints' stories that have preceded it but certainly casts suspicion on some of the narratives that he has related: "Thus farre of the Irishe Sainctes. Of the whyche, as some of them are to bee esteemed right vertuous and godlye menne, so other of them are to bee suspected, as persons rather holye by the superstitious opinion of the people, than endued with any suche knowledge of true godlynesse and syncere Relygion, as are woorthye to be Registred in the number of those that of right ought to passe for sayntes, as by certayne late writers may appear"(*Irish,* 141).

The "certayne late writers" to whom Holinshed refers are Foxe and Bale (as noted in the margin), implying that if the Irish saints are not the Protestant martyrs included in the *Acts and Monuments* or Bale's *Examinations* (and of course they are not), they probably are not saints. Thus Holinshed's voice supersedes Campion's without canceling it, and both Catholic and Protestant views are presented, however uneasily, to the reader side by side.

Holinshed concludes the first book with a history of the Scandinavian invasions and a brief but unrelated explanation of the Irish process of installing bishops. The end of the first book is particularly disjointed, jumping without transition or explanation from the history of the early Irish saints to an account of Norwegian and Danish invasions to the election of Irish bishops. While the organizational weakness of this section supports Holinshed's claim that he lacked time and resources in compiling the Irish history, its fragmentary nature cannot be attributed solely to Holinshed's haste, since the format follows that of Campion's text. What this section of the history does suggest is that Holinshed lacked sufficient resources to fill out Campion's work.

The second book of the "Historie of Ireland" relates the story of Henry II's invasion and conquest of Ireland and continues until the death of Henry VII. The section that describes Henry II's conquest, based on Giraldus Cambrensis's *Expugnatio Hibernia* (*Conquest of Ireland*), is a quickly paced and interesting narrative, reflecting Giraldus's own considerable gifts as a storyteller. In the opening chapter, King Dermote Macmurche of Leinster seduces and abducts the wife of King Morice of Meath. The ensuing quarrel results in Dermote's abandonment by his subjects; the loss of his kingdom; and his flight to England, where he promises Henry II his kingdom in exchange for military support and a portion of his lost lands. Henry's willingness to help the King of Leinster; Dermote's match of his daughter and only heir to Richard Strangbow, Earl of Pembroke; and his promise of Irish land to the Welsh lords Robert Fitz Stephans and Maurice Fitzgerald in exchange for help in regaining his kingdom set the stage for the Irish conquest.

To avoid the impression that Henry II's invasion was a self-interested land grab brought about by an English alliance with a lecher and a traitor, Holinshed, following Campion, presents the Irish conquest as a holy war, authorized by the English pope Adrian and confirmed and ratified by his successor, Alexander, to insure that true religion is returned to Ireland: "Although Christ was there taught and beleeved, yet the multitude being a furious and savage generation, were growen to suche a licentious and shamefull kinde of libertie, making no accounte of the necesarie pointes of doctrine, more than served their sensuall and wilfull lustes, that it was greatly to bee doubted, least they would at length utterly abandon Christianitie, and give themselves over to a beastly order of living, nothing agreeable with the lawes and rites of other people that professed Christes Religion" (*Irish,* 154–55).

To reinforce the argument that the Irish conquest was divinely preordained, Holinshed includes prophecies of the conquest attributed to the four great Irish saints, Patrick, Brachan, Colme, and Moling, as well as a prophecy of Merlin's that "the sixt shall overthrow the Walles of Irelande, and againe five portions shall be brought into one," the sixth referring to Henry II and the five portions to the five Irish kingdoms (*Irish,* 169). The narrative's depiction of the Irish clergy's acquiescence to the invasion as God's rightful punishment for Ireland's sinfulness is a further justification for Henry's claim to Ireland, as is the careful notation that Henry's first act after conquering Ireland was to reform the Irish church, clearing it of "many inordinate and heynous customs" and abolishing its "enormous abuses."

The English conquest also reintroduces the theme that Ireland's chronic internal squabbling is the primary cause of its susceptibility to frequent attacks. Henry's invasion, like preceding ones depicted in the Irish history, greatly benefits from the Irish leaders' inability to cooperate among themselves. For example, when the Irish kings sue Fitz Stephans for peace, the Welsh conqueror "marvelled much at the follie of those Princes, who, to satisfie their displeasure and malice, had opened such a gappe to their owne destruction, not considering howe the subjectes whome they had schooled to breake their allegaunce aneynst [against] theyr naturall Prince, the King of Leynister, would not be as ready to rebell against the King of Connagh" (*Irish,* 158). The tendency of Irish leaders to place personal revenge above the common good is also demonstrated in King Dermot's behavior after regaining his lands with the help of his English and Welsh allies. Intending to become king of all Ireland, he wastes Meath and Dublin and invades Connaght. Dermot's destruction of his neighbor's kingdoms precipitates even greater English control of Ireland. His death results in the inheritance of his vast landholdings by his Anglo-Norman son-in-law Strangbow and the consequent establishment of the great Anglo-Irish palatinate system in Ireland, a scourge to the Gaelic Irish and a thorn in the side of every English monarch to follow.

The account of the English conquest ends with John Lackland's disastrous visit to Ireland, an example of cross-cultural miscommunication witnessed by Giraldus Cambrensis himself. As the story relates, Henry II awarded his son John lordship of Ireland, and the 12-year-old prince subsequently traveled to the country to receive tribute from the Irish kings. The Irish nobility, bearing rich gifts, greeted the young prince and "made unto the child, their most sovereign lorde, the most joy and gladnesse that might bee, and though rudely, yet lovingly, and after the usage of their country offered to kisse him aftersuch a friendly familiarity as they were accustomed to shewe towardes the Princes at home." When John's Norman guards seize the nobles by their beards and hair and cast them out of the Prince's presence, the grievously insulted Irish declare their refusal to honor a "peevish and insolent" boy as their sovereign and instigate a rebellion "to stand in defence of their auncient liberties" (*Irish,* 190). Relations between the English and the Irish steadily decline from this point on, and the history that follows the conquest depicts a cycle of Irish rebellions and English efforts to subdue those rebellions; infighting among the English and Irish alike; political appointments; marriages, births, and deaths; and the occasional earthquake, famine, or pestilence.

After the focused and fast-paced narrative of the conquest, the Irish history degenerates into a traditional chronicle format in which unrelated events are listed without cause, effect, or analysis. Its primary interest lies in the portrayal of a gradually developing sense of an Anglo-Irish identity independent of English influence. The descendants of the conquerors become involved in a series of rebellions against English rule as they come to identify more with Ireland and less with England. In 1315 the Anglo-Irish lords join forces with the Gaelic Irish to overthrow English rule and threaten to rebel again during Edward III's reign, when the king revokes all liberties granted in Ireland. During the reign of Henry VI "a great fellowship of English Rebells" join the forces of the Irish lord Mogoghigam in another attempt to overthrow English rule.

The final pages of the second book trace the gradual loss of English influence in Ireland, the shrinkage of the Pale, and the return of Gaelic-Irish influence and rule to Ulster, Munster, and Connaught, primarily as a result of England's preoccupation with its own civil wars. Those pages devoted to the reign of Henry VII highlight Ireland's role in the rebellions of the Yorkist pretenders Lambert Simnel and Perkin Warbeck as well as England's attempts to reassert its authority in Ireland under the

lieutenantship of Henry, duke of York, later Henry VIII, whose reign is
the subject of Stanyhurst's third book.

   Like Holinshed's Irish history, Stanyhurst's third book of the Irish
history is based on Campion's *Historie of Ireland.* Stanyhurst adds extensive new material to his work, primarily anecdotes and details of personality. Ostensibly a history of Ireland during the reign of Henry VIII, the
text deals primarily with the fortunes of the Fitzgeralds of Kildare,
whom Stanyhurst served as a tutor. The Fitzgerald family, one of the
oldest and most powerful of the Anglo-Norman dynasties, had succeeded over the centuries in establishing a palatinate in southern Ireland
and produced two of the most notorious of the sixteenth-century Irish
rebellions against the English, the Silken Thomas and the Desmond.
The Kildare branch of the family had also produced several outstanding
leaders within the Pale community, including two lords deputy of Ireland, Garret Mor and Garret Og, who also happened to be the grandfather and father of the Silken Thomas rebellion's leader, Thomas
Fitzgerald. Lasting from 1534 to 1535, the Silken Thomas rebellion
succeeded in driving the English from most of eastern and southern Ireland before the rebels were defeated by Henry VIII's troops. After
Thomas's capture, Henry imprisoned and executed most of the Fitzgerald leaders, effectively obliterating the Kildare branch of the clan.

   Stanyhurst himself would have had a personal interest in the rebellion for a number of reasons. His father, James, was one of the youths
taken hostage by Thomas Fitzgerald during the siege of Dublin, and his
employer, Gerald Fitzgerald, eleventh earl of Kildare, was Thomas's
half-brother, a relationship that almost cost him his life. Stanyhurst,
who devotes a good portion of both his description and his history of
Ireland to defending the Fitzgerald dynasty, is put in the awkward position of depicting one of the most notorious and most successful rebellions in sixteenth-century Irish history without offending either his
employer or, more importantly, the Crown. His near success in carrying
off this task is marred only by the expurgation of a section of his history
that consists primarily of slanderous gossip about the Fitzgeralds' enemies Archbishop John Allen and his secretary, John Allen (no relation).

   Stanyhurst depicts the Silken Thomas rebellion as the result of a
series of tragic misunderstandings fueled by the machinations of the
Fitzgeralds' enemies as well as of self-serving counselors and Gaelic aris-
tocrats who preyed on the inexperience and naïveté of a headstrong and
immature young man. The account of how Thomas was mistakenly led
to believe that his father, the earl, had been executed is full of surprising

plot turns and coincidences. Stanyhurst claims that the servants and friends of the former and soon-to-be-reinstated lord deputy of Ireland, William Skeffington, circulated letters spreading rumors of the earl's death. One such letter came into the hands of a priest, who "for haste hurled it among other papers in the chimneis end of his chamber, meaning to peruse it better at more leysure." That night one of Thomas's retainers happened to lodge with that priest, and in the morning "when he rose for some paper, to drawe on his strayte stockings, and as the Divell woulde, he hit upon the letter, bare it away in the heele of his stocke, no earthly thing misdeeming." At night, the retainer discovered the letter in his stocking, "beganne to poare on the writing which notified the Earle his death and the apprehension of the Lord Thomas." The retainer immediately brought the letter to James Delahide, Thomas's principal counselor, who in turn gave it to Thomas, "and withall putting fire to flaxe, before he dived to the bottome of this treacherie, hee was contented to swim on the skum and froth thereof, as well by soothing up the tenour of the letter, as by inciting Lorde Thomas to open rebellion, cloaking the odious name of treason with the zealous revengment of his fathers wrong full execution, and with the warie defence of his own person" (*Irish*, 261–62). Stanyhurst thus blames the older man for pushing Thomas into open rebellion over the contents of a letter that too late are proven to be false.

Although he does not excuse Thomas's actions, Stanyhurst often mitigates their seriousness. For example, Stanyhurst claims that the bloody execution of John Allen, Archbishop of Dublin, was a tragic misunderstanding because Thomas had only intended to take him prisoner. Thomas's instructions, "Bir wem e boddeagh," which Stanyhurst translates as "Take the Churle from me" or "Away with the Churle," were taken by his followers as an order to kill the archbishop, and they "without further delay, brayned and hackt hym in gobbets." Stanyhurst, no admirer of Allen's, notes that the archbishop may have indirectly caused his own death, claiming that Allen, an enemy of the Fitzgeralds', was "not unlike to have promoted their accusations, and to have bin a forger of the letter before mentioned, which turned to his final destruction" (*Irish*, 269). Stanyhurst thus relieves Thomas of the primary guilt for the archbishop's death.

Even the rebellion's failure is portrayed as tragic, the result of a series of betrayals and broken promises rather than any military weaknesses. Thomas's own foster brother, Christopher Parese, betrayed Thomas's stronghold of Maynooth Castle to the English in exchange for money.

Again, Stanyhurst's gift for anecdote and direct speech render the incident a fascinating account of personalities and motives. After entering the stronghold, Lord Deputy Skeffington asked Parese what benefits Thomas had bestowed on him so that he might better know how to reward him. The unsuspecting Parese, "supposing the more he recited the better should he be rewarded, left not untolde the meanest good turne that ever he received at his lords hands. 'Why Parese,' quoth the Deputie, 'couldest thou finde in thine hearte to betray his Castell, that hath bin so good Lord unto thee? Truly, thou that art so hollow to him, wilt never be true to us' "(*Irish*, 279). The lord deputy then ordered that Parese be given his money and his head struck off.

Even the English apprehension of Thomas and the rest of the Fitzgerald clan is portrayed as an act of betrayal. When the promised aid from continental Catholic rulers never materialized, Thomas finally turned himself in with the understanding that he would be granted a full pardon if he sailed to England. "To the end that no treacherie might have bene misdeemed of eyther side," the English and rebel leaders "both receyved the Sacrament openly in the campe, as an infallible seale of the covenants and conditions of either part agreed" (*Irish*, 283). Against the advice of his counselors, Thomas dismissed his troops and sailed to England, where he was immediately thrown into the Tower. On order of the king, Leonard Grey, who became lord deputy after the death of Skeffington in 1535, then arrested and sent to England Thomas's five uncles, three of whom were apprehended at a banquet that Grey held in their honor and the remaining two "roundly snatched up in villages hard by." Although three uncles had openly opposed their nephew's rebellion, all five, along with Thomas, were drawn, hanged, and quartered on 3 February 1536. Thomas's father, the earl, had already died in prison.

On the question of Grey's betrayal of both Thomas and his uncles, Stanyhurst, usually an outspoken critic of unethical behavior, remains silent, obviously because Grey's actions were ordered by the king himself. In his depiction of the blasphemy of a broken pledge sealed by a sacrament and in a banquet host's betrayal of his invited guests, Stanyhurst lets the events speak for themselves. By no means does Stanyhurst ever reveal any sympathy for the rebellion, and his text is filled with frequent interjections such as "For sacred is the name of a king, and odious is the name of a rebellion: the one from heaven derived, and by God shielded, the other in hell forged, and by the Deauville executed." Nevertheless, he maintains his loyalty to the Fitzgeralds throughout his narrative, and although he is never complimentary in his depiction of Thomas as a headstrong and foolish boy, his treatment of him is noticeably gentler than his treatment of the other rebels. Even in his closing commentary, Stanyhurst adamantly defends the loyalty of all earls of Kildare, an honor held by the eldest heir of the house of Fitzgerald. He speciously argues that Thomas, even as eldest and heir, never actually held the title, and therefore "ever since the conquest, that notwithstanding all the presumptions of treason wherewith any earle of kildare could either faintly be suspected or vehemently charged, yet there was never any earl of that house read or heard of that bare armour in the field against his Prince." Stanyhurst claims to maintain this point "not as barrister hired to plead theyr cause, but as a Chronicler mooved to tell the truth" (*Irish*, 285–86).

Unlike Holinshed and, later, Hooker, Stanyhurst focuses on personalities and causation in his depiction of historical action, creating a fascinating account, reminiscent of Greek tragedy, of the Silken Thomas rebellion. According to Stanyhurst's narrative, the Silken Thomas rebellion is the result of Thomas's own hubris combined with a series of causally related events careening toward a disastrous end. An inveterate gossip and outspoken critic, Stanyhurst uses lively anecdotes, extensive direct quotation, linguistic flamboyance, and detailed evaluation of personalities to lend his text a vibrancy and interest notably lacking in the first two books of the "History of Ireland." Stanyhurst's style is highly colloquial, and the humor inherent in much of his description helps to break the tension of a decidedly tragic narrative. In describing the anger of Silken Thomas, he refers to him as "frying in his grease." When the rebels are turned back in their seige of Dublin, Stanyhurst quotes them as realizing that "no butter could stick on their bread in that parte of the citie." He describes the expert marksmanship of Dick Stanton, one of Dublin's defenders, by describing how "he galde dyvers of the rebelles as they woulde skippe from house to house, by causing some of them, with his peece, to carrie theyr erraundes in their buttockes" (*Irish*, 273).

Stanyhurst's penchant for gossip and a good anecdote may have caused the third book of the Irish history to become the only portion of the 1577 *Chronicles* to be questioned by the government and expurgated. Confusion exists over the actual motives for the cancellation of leaves 2E6 through F7.[3] Historical records demonstrate that on 5 December 1577, the Privy Council issued two letters concerning Stanyhurst's history because it contained "many thinges . . . falcelie [falsely] recited and contrarie to the ancient records" (*APC*, x:114–1150).

One letter instructed John Alymer, bishop of London and an official often charged with supervision of the press, to summon the printer of the *Chronicles* to find out how many copies had been printed, how many were sold in Ireland, and how many remained unsold. He was also instructed to forbid the printer from printing or selling any more copies. The other letter was sent to Stanyhurst's employer, Gerald Fitzgerald, the eleventh earl of Kildare, requiring him to send them "his servant" Stanyhurst, who would then learn their pleasure. The Acts of the Privy Council from 13 January 13, 1578 state of Stanyhurst that "forasmuche as the compyler thereof hathe shewed the cause how he was induced to those errors, and offereth to reforme them, his Lordship is willed, after signification made unto him from the Lord Treasurer that those faultes are reformed, he shall suffer them to passe and to be sould notwithstanding the former restrainte" (*APC*, x:142). No further information on the canceling and substitution of the 1577 text exists, nor does any order for revision or list of expurgators survive as they do in the case of the censorship of the 1587 *Chronicles*.

Because of this, Anne Castanien has argued that the 1577 cancellands were not necessarily the result of the Privy Council's actions. With regard to the first cancellands, which include the beginning of the history, the replacement leaves do not contract or expunge the previous text but rather expand the history, adding new details and material (Castanien, 91–122). The second cancellands involve the removal of some malicious gossip concerning Archbishop John Allen and his secretary; Stanyhurst accuses the secretary of pandering his wife to the archbishop. Whereas Castanien believes that the removal may have been the result of in-house editing rather than the council's order of revision, other critics maintain that the passage on Allen was indeed excised by order of the Council (*Irish*, xvi-xvii).

1587 "Historie of Ireland"

Although the 1577 edition of the "Chronicles of Ireland" can certainly be viewed as a moderate and even positive presentation of Ireland's history and culture, sympathetic to the cause of legal reform as a solution to Ireland's problems, the 1587 edition is a far more problematic, confusing, and essentially self-contradictory text. Except for the substitution of Hooker's heavily annotated translation of Giraldus Cambrensis's *Conquest of Ireland* for Holinshed's account of the Anglo-Norman conquest, the 1587 edition preserves the entirety of Holinshed's and Stanyhurst's 1577 Irish contributions, unabridged and unchanged, side by side with "The Supplie to the Irish Chronicle," John Hooker's vituperative history of the Irish from 1546 to 1586. Other changes to the 1577 "Chronicles of Ireland" are fairly minor, consisting mainly of typographical, spelling, and punctuation modifications and the inclusion of chapter headings. As in the rest of the *Chronicles,* the 1577 woodcuts are also deleted.

Hooker dedicated his translation of the *Conquest of Ireland* to Sir Walter Raleigh, who had played a significant role in Irish affairs through his involvement in the suppression of the second Desmond Rebellion (1579–1586). In the dedication, Hooker explains Giraldus Cambrensis's importance as the father of Anglo-Irish history and his desire to give Giraldus the recognition that he deserves (*Chronicles*, 6:109). A Welshman, Giraldus had traveled to Ireland in the train of Prince John in 1185 and later wrote the *Topographia Hiberniae* (Topography of Ireland) and the *Conquest of Ireland,* both of which influenced the *Chronicles'* "Description of Ireland" and the "Historie of Ireland." Giraldus had other ties to Ireland as well. He belonged to the Fitzgerald family that had played a key role in the conquest of Ireland and later became one of the most powerful and influential of the Anglo-Irish families in medieval and early modern Ireland. This was the same family that Stanyhurst wrote of in his 1577 "Description" and "Booke Three" and that Hooker treated in his account in the "Supplie" of the Desmond rebellion.

The 1587 translation of Giraldus Cambrensis's *Conquest of Ireland* is a far more detailed and extensive narrative than the account provided in the 1577 *Chronicles,* which in comparison reads like a cursory outline. Because of Giraldus's moralistic commentary and his inclusion of lengthy speeches presented as direct quotations, the 1587 record of the Irish conquest is considerably longer than the 1577 account, yet this does not necessarily work to the text's disadvantage. The speeches, primarily exhortations to action, give the text a liveliness and immediacy that the 1577 version lacks. Perhaps the most noteworthy difference between the two editions' history of the conquest concerns the presentation of its underlying motives. Because Holinshed uses Campion's adaption of Giraldus as an outline for his history, he follows Campion's lead in rearranging Giraldus's text to make it appear that Henry II sought the pope's approval before invading Ireland, presenting the conquest as an event sanctioned by both God and church. The 1577 edition locates Henry's petition at the very beginning of the text, thus implying that Henry conquered Ireland only after the action was authorized by Rome and primarily for the purpose of cleansing the corruption of the Irish ecclesiastical and secular governments. In Giraldus, the reference to Henry requesting the Pope's permission does not appear until chapter 5 of the second book, after Henry has already invaded Ireland, and Henry's request is portrayed as an afterthought sought to justify an action already taken. Reference to the corruption of the Irish church, which Holinshed, again following Campion's example, places at the beginning of his history, does not appear until chapter 34 of book 1 in Giraldus's text.

Filled with explanations, digressions, and analyses of the conquest of Ireland, Giraldus's narrative clarifies the motives and behavior of the various actors in this pivotal event. Hooker's copious notes at the end of each chapter offer helpful clarifications of historical events, explanations of the numerous classical references with which Giraldus sprinkles his text, and skeptical dismissals of the numerous marvels and supernatural events that Giraldus included in his work. Hooker's early modern Protestant commentary on the medieval churchman's narrative creates a lively dialogue, as both author and translator were not averse to expressing their opinions on anything and everything. Since both saw Irish history as a continuous manifestation of God's justice, their divergent views on the roles of church and state offer some interesting insights into the differences between a medieval English and an early modern English interpretation of historical facts. Giraldus attributes the problems that plagued Henry II's later reign to his choice to wage war on Ireland for his own self-aggrandizement rather than take up the Crusade for God and church. (*Chronicles*, 6:224). The failure of the English to effect a full and final conquest on Ireland he credits to their lack of gratitude to God, manifested by their treatment of the church (6:227). Hooker, on the other hand, presents God's wrath as a punishment for those who would disobey their king rather than their church. He often and vehemently declares that the failure of every Irish rebellion is due to God's wrath over the fact that the Irish would rise up against God's anointed. The divergent viewpoints of the author and the translator reflect their own specific historical situations. For the medieval priest Giraldus, the church represents God's authority on earth; for the English Protestant Hooker, the sovereign does. Therefore, those who cross the church are punished in Giraldus's narrative, and those who oppose their sovereign are castigated in Hooker's.

Another example of the textual dialogue between author and translator, twelfth-century churchman and sixteenth-century Protestant, appears in Hooker's updated histories of the descendants of the various personalities featured in *Conquest*. These interpolations offer a provocative counterpoint to Giraldus's account of the conquest as well as to Stanyhurst's 1577 presentation of the Anglo Irish, especially since a number of these descendants went "native" and even played pivotal roles in rebellions against the English Crown a few centuries later. For instance, Hooker notes of Philip of Barrie's descendants that "nothing degenerating from their first ancestor, have from age and to age beene noble and valiant gentlemen, and who for their fidelitie and good services, were advanced to honour and made viscounts, and in that title of honor doo continue still. But would to God they were not so nuzled, rooted, and altogither seasoned in Irishrie! The name and honor being only English, all the rest for the most part Irish" (*Chronicles*, 6:207). Another example of this revisionist appraisal appears in response to Giraldus's celebration of the Fitzgeralds' role in the conquest. Hooker, who had little respect for the clan, offers a caustic commentary on their later role in Irish history:

> It is very true, that these Geraldines even ever since have continued in this land of Ireland, and did daily grow and increase to much honour: there being at this instant two houses advanced to the titles of earldoms, and sundrie to the estates of barons. And so long as they continued in the steps of their ancestors, they were not so honourable as terrible to the Irish nation: but when they leaving English government, like the loose life of that viperous nation, then they brought in coine and liverie, and a number of many other Irish and divelish impositions, which hath beene the ruine of their honour, the losse of their credit and in the end will be the overthrow of all their houses and families. (*Chronicles*, 6:198)

Whereas much of Giraldus's text is a running complaint about the conquerors' poor treatment of the church and the deceitful nature of the Irish, his closing commentary on the "the full and final conquest of Ireland" includes a cogent analysis of the conquest's failures, including a stinging critique of the Normans, whom he declares are unfit for leadership:

> They received great interteinment and were liberally rewarded, and left no meanes unsought how they might rule the rost, beare the sway, and be advanced unto high estate and honour. In these things they were the first and formost, but to serve in hosting, to incounter with the enimie, to defend the publike state, & to follow anie martiall affaires, they were the last and furthest off. (*Chronicles*, 6:229)

Giraldus blames the continual rebellion in Ireland on the Anglo Normans' ill treatment of the Irish and their betrayal of Irish trust. He suggests that the conquest would prove far more successful if kindness and good example were displayed toward those Irish who willingly subjected themselves to English government and firm and swift punishment administered to those who rebel. He also notes that his own countrymen, the Welsh, would make superior soldiers to the Normans currently stationed in Ireland.

Giraldus's mastery of the anecdote; his fascination with visions, prophecies, dreams, and other supernatural phenomena; his perceptive depiction of character and motivation; his employment of direct quotation to heighten the drama of a scene; and his love of moral commentary all create a lively and memorable portrait of Henry II's conquest of Ireland. Hooker's translation preserves the simplicity and directness of the original, and his extensive notes not only clarify and amplify the medieval text but also provide a fascinating insight into the various concerns and problems that still haunted English-Irish relations four hundred years after the conquest. The imposition of English culture on the Gaelic Irish; the threat that the great Anglo-Irish lords posed to the English Crown; the continual fear of rebellion and violence; the attempts to impose the forms of the English Church on the Irish Church, albeit the English Church that later became Protestant—all these concerns of Giraldus's time were still pressing issues at the end of the sixteenth century, as Hooker's "Supplie to the Irish Chronicle" demonstrates.

Dedicated to Sir John Perot, lord deputy of Ireland at the time of its publication, "The Supplie of this Irish Chronicle, Continued from the Death of King Henry VIII, 1546, until this Present Yeare 1586" continues from the point where Stanyhurst's 1577 Irish history ends, the death of Henry VIII. Hooker's text deals with a particularly turbulent time in Irish history. Land confiscation and the plantation system contributed to growing Irish discontent in areas such as the northeast and Munster, and the growing power of the central English government provoked resentment and active resistance.[4] Furthermore, the Continent's political and religious tensions found expression within Ireland as the major rebellions of this period brought to the forefront the issue of religious allegiance. Strengthened with financial and military support from Catholic Europe, a number of Gaelic-Irish and Anglo-Irish nobles fought to free if not Ireland, then at least their own principalities from English Protestant rule. These numerous and often interrelated rebellions threw Ireland into a state of anarchy for most of Elizabeth's reign.

The Irish uprisings also fed England's fear that a foreign power could indeed use Ireland to threaten England's security (Meyers, 6–7).

Like Stanyhurst, Hooker drew on his personal experiences in Ireland for his contributions to the *Chronicles,* and this is particularly apparent in the "Supplie." Hooker first arrived in Ireland as a solicitor for the military commander and colonist Sir Peter Carew, enabling Carew to claim title to the barony of Idrone and the lands of Sir Christopher Cheever. Not only was this an example of the growing number of attempts by English adventurers to seize lands by both legitimate and illegitimate means, but its success also led to Carew's commencement of proceedings to lay claim to lands occupied by the Butlers, one of the most ancient and powerful Anglo-Irish noble families. The Butlers' violent resistance to Carew's claims led to a great land war that threatened to devastate Munster as much as Ulster had been devastated in the conflict with Shane O'Neill.[5] Carew's political influence helped Hooker obtain a seat in the 1568 Irish Parliament as the representative of Athenry, although Hooker was later driven from that Parliament after he made a speech particularly offensive to the Opposition. Hooker's chaotic experiences in the Irish House of Commons led to the writing and publication of his most famous work, the "Order and Usage of the Keeping of a Parliament in England."

Although it was not originally written for the *Chronicles,* Hooker chose to include the "Order and Usage" in the "Supplie" directly after his account of his experiences in the Irish Parliament, although his reasons for doing so remain unclear. The "Order and Usage," the first published description of Parliament and its lawmaking procedures, was originally dedicated to Sir William Fitzwilliam, lord deputy of Ireland from 1571 to 1575, and was issued in London in pamphlet form in 1572. Around 1575 it was issued again but this time dedicated to the mayor and civic leaders of Exeter, Hooker's native city. The "Order and Usage" provides a firsthand description of the Elizabethan Parliament's structure, composition, and policies, laying out the degrees of Parliament, the officers and their various responsibilities, the proper meeting time of parliament, and the proper procedures.[6]

Unlike Stanyhurst, whose affection for his native land, if not all of its inhabitants, permeates his contributions to the *Chronicles,* Hooker openly and often articulates a real hostility toward all things Irish, and in his epistle dedicatory to Sir Walter Raleigh, which appears before his translation of Giraldus Cambrensis, he bewails the fact that he has allowed himself to be prevailed on to write a history of Ireland:

A countrie, the more barren of good things, the more replenished with
actions of bloud, murther, and lothsome outrages; which to anie good
reader are greevous & irkesome to be read & considered, much more for
anie man to pen and set downe in writing, and to reduce into an historie.
Which hath beene some cause whie I was alienated and utterlie discouraged to intermedle therein: for being earnestlie requested, by reason of
my some acquaintance with the maners and conditions of that nation
during my short abode therein, to continue the historie of that land . . . I
found no matter of an historie woorthie to be recorded: but rather a
tragedie of cruelties to be abhorred, and no historie of good things to be
followed: and therefore I gave the matter over, and was fullie resolved
not at all to have intermedled therewith. Neverthelesse, being againe
verie earnestlie requested . . . then (but with an evill will) I entred into it.
(*Chronicles*, 6:103)

Hooker's "evil will" on entering his project appears in his continual contempt for the Irish, both Gaelic and Anglo, throughout his work.

A comparison of Stanyhurst's and Hooker's contributions to the *Irish
Chronicles* reflects the varying and often conflicting solutions to the "Irish
problem" circulated during Elizabeth's reign and in doing so reveals the
tensions at this time among the three cultural communities in Ireland:
the Gaelic Irish, the Anglo Irish, and the New English. Legal reform
was characteristically advocated by the Anglo Irish, who were, for the
most part, descendants of twelfth-century Anglo-Norman settlers and
whose interests lay in protecting their own political power and landholdings. Richard Stanyhurst's "Description of Ireland" and "Third
Booke" of the Irish history reflect this point of view. Conquest and colonization were favored by the New English, those men who came to
prominence as a consequence of the renewed English intervention in Ireland in the sixteenth century. As Clare Carroll and Vincent Carey note in
their introduction to Richard Beacon's *Solon his follie* (1594), "New English soldiers and settlers, rivals of the Old English for positions and
land, staked their claim to power in Ireland upon the exercise of arms
and appropriation of land; hence, conquest and colonization were their
preferred policies."[7] For this reason the New English made little effort to
distinguish between the Anglo-Irish inhabitants of Ireland, especially
those who lived beyond the Pale, and the "Meere Irish," or Gaelic-Irish
inhabitants. To do so would be to acknowledge the Anglo Irish as fellow
Englishmen and therefore undermine the New English colonizers'
claims to the lands and power held by the Anglo Irish. Hooker's "Supplie" falls squarely into this later camp and as such serves as an apology

for Elizabeth's policy of placing New English colonists in Irish administrative positions traditionally held by the Anglo Irish.

Hooker's "Supplie" is a history of violence, rebellion, civil war, and
bloodshed, and one would be hard-pressed to recognize the Ireland that
Stanyhurst had so fondly described in his contributions to the Irish
"Chronicles." Hooker, like most Elizabethan writers and commentators
on Ireland, saw the Gaelic Irish as treacherous savages, a "wicked, enf-
frenated [violent], barbarous, and unfaithful people." Unlike Stanyhurst, he did not believe in their reformability, nor does he make any
real distinctions between the Anglo Irish who lived beyond the Pale and
the Gaelic Irish in his text. Though Hooker does differentiate between
the Pale residents and the Anglo Irish beyond the Pale, emphasizing the
loyalty of the Pale residents to their sovereign and faulting them only in
their complaints against the cess, a tax used to support the increasing
number of royal troops, he tends to lump all those living beyond the
Pale, both Gaelic and Anglo, into the same category. He refers to both
groups as "Irish," as exemplified in his list of "Irish Lords," which consists entirely of Anglo-Irish families (*Chronicles*, 6:413).

As far as Hooker was concerned, these ancient Anglo-Irish families
were the cause of most of Ireland's problems. He portrays them as disordered, violent, and vengeful and plays on their assimilation into
Gaelic culture, a point that Stanyhurst is always careful to minimize.
Hooker levels his most disparaging criticism at the Fitzgerald earls of
Desmond and the Butler earls of Ormond. Their land disputes, which
wasted most of Limerick in the 1560s and proved to be the last private
war between Tudor noblemen, is portrayed in the "Supplie" as "the dis-
turbance of the whole realme, the spoile of the whole countrie, and the
onelie case of great murthers, bloudshed, and undooing of manie people" (*Chronicles*, 6:338). Hooker details the "sundrie grievous complaints" against Sir Edmund Butler and his brothers for "sundrie routs
and riots, spoiles and outrages which they were charged to have doone
upon hir majesties' subjects" (6:362). The palatine of Gerald Fitzgerald, fourteenth earl of Desmond, is "a sanctuarie for all lewd and
wicked persons" (6:384).

As in Stanyhurst's "Thirde Booke of the Irish Historie," the focal
point of Hooker's "Supplie" is a rebellion led by the Fitzgeralds, but
Stanyhurst's and Hooker's points of view are strikingly different.
Whereas Stanyhurst's account of the Silken Thomas rebellion has all the
elements of a Greek tragedy, in which misunderstanding, tragic coinci-
dence, and Thomas Fitzgerald's fatal flaw of hubris lead to a heart-

breaking disaster, Hooker's narrative of the Desmond rebellion reveals only contempt and hatred for the leaders of that debacle.

In 1579, Garret Fitzgerald, then earl of Desmond, with the aid of Italian and Spanish soldiers financed by Pope Gregory XIII raised a rebellion that almost succeeded, pushing the English out of Munster and most of Leinster. The English responded with a scorched-earth policy, destroying the 1580 harvest, slaughtering cattle, and finally massacring the surrendered Italian-Spanish forces on the Dingle Peninsula in 1580. The countryside was so wasted that even the English army could not find sufficient provisions during the campaign. By 1583, the rebellion had been completely suppressed and Desmond himself murdered by his own people on a mountain in Kerry.

Hooker employs the hydra as his dominant image for the Desmond rebellion, and as each of its leaders is captured and executed, he systematically compares his demise to the cutting off of one of the hydra's many heads. For example, when James Fitzgerald, the earl of Desmond's brother, is captured and executed by Walter Raleigh, Hooker notes, "[A]nd thus the pestilent hydra hath lost an other of his heads" (*Chronicles*, 6:433). After relating how the head of the earl's other brother John is sent to Dublin and his body hung by the heels on a gibbet and set on the north gate of Cork, Hooker again employs the image: "And thus have you the third head of the venomous Hydra cut off, who had his just reward and merit, if not too good for so villanous & bloudie a traitor" (6:446). Hooker describes the earl's own death by decapitation as an example of the "mightie hand of God against traitors and rebels," noting that it was uncertain whether the earl's body was buried or "devoured by the wild beasts" (6:459).

Indeed, the use of beast imagery to describe the Anglo Irish and Gaelic Irish is one of the hallmarks of Hooker's text, and he reiterates certain set phrases that depict animals returning to their natural state, no matter how vile, to depict the irredeemability of Ireland's inhabitants and the futility of trying to "improve" their lot. Hooker's use of animal similes and metaphors underscores the deep differences between his point of view toward the Irish and Stanyhurst's. In his continual metaphorical depictions of both the Gaelic Irish and Anglo Irish as bestial, Hooker emphasizes their innate wickedness and resistance to improvement and therefore justifies the use of force and aggression in dealing with them: "For withdraw the sword and forbeare correction, deale with them in courtesie and intreate them gentlie, if they can take anie advantage, they will surelie skip out; and as the dog to his vomit, and the sow to the durt & puddle, they will returne to their old and former insolencie, rebellion, and disobedience" (6:369).

Hooker's favorite phrases, "the dog to his vomit" and "swine to their dirt and puddles," appear to have been borrowed from 2 Peter 2:21–24: "It would have been better for them never to have learnt the way of uprightness, than to learn it and then desert the holy commandment that was entrusted to them. What they have done is exactly as the proverb rightly says: The dog goes back to its vomit and: As soon as the sow has been washed, it wallows in the mud." These images emphasize Hooker's firm belief in the inherent treachery and rebelliousness of the Irish and indeed his hatred of anything Irish as a filthy abomination. Furthermore, the phrases' biblical origin in Peter's reference to those who deny Christ in order to return to "the pollution of the world" underscores Hooker's argument that Ireland's rebellion against English sovereignty was a sinful rejection of the divine plan. The phrases appear twice in his description of Munster's inhabitants: "[Y]et as swine delighting in their dirt and puddles, [they] contented themselves rather with a beggerlie life to be miserable, than in dutifull obedience to be at peace and assured" (*Chronicles,* 6:328). Again, later in the text Hooker expands on this simile when referring to the Irish response to the arrival of Sir John Perot, then lord president of Munster: "They heard no sooner of his comming, but as a sort of wasps they fling out, and revolting from their former feigned obedience, became open rebelles and traitors under James Fitzmoris an archtraitor, and as dogs they returne to their vomit , and as swine to their durt and puddles" (*Chronicles*, 6:369). To borrow a phrase from Shakespeare, in Hooker's eyes the Anglo Irish and Gaelic Irish both were devils, born devils, "on whose nature / Nurture can never stick."

Hooker also relies on animal proverbs and tales to drive home his argument that the inhabitants of Ireland are inherently evil and unredeemable. Again, these proverbs and tales are repeated at various points throughout the text to emphasize his point. Though at first Hooker's reiteration of the same images may seem to reveal a certain lack of imagination, the overall effect is to blur distinctions between the Gaelic Irish and the Anglo Irish, since he indiscriminately uses these images in reference to both groups. For example, in his narrative of the Anglo-Irish baron of Lexnew's son, Patrick, who was raised and educated in England but on returning home to Ireland joined the ranks of the Desmond rebels, he relates the proverb of the ape in purple velvet and the folktale of Jupiter's cat:

And therefore they maie be verie well resembled to an ape, which (as the common proverbe is) an ape is but an ape, albeit he be clothed in purple and velvet, even so this wicked impe. For notwithstanding he was trained up in the court of England, sworne servant unto hir majestie, in good favour and countenance in the court, and apparelled according to his degree, and dailie nurtured and brought up in all civilitie: he was no sooner come home, but awaie with his English attires, and on with his brogs, his shirt, and other Irish rags, being become as verie a traitor as the veriest knave of them, & so for the most part they are all, as dailie experience teacheth, dissemble they never so much to the contrarie. For like as Jupiters cat, let hir be transformed to never so faire a ladie, and let hir be never so well attired and accompanied with the best ladies, let hir be never so well esteemed and honored: yet if the mouse come once in hir sight, she will be a cat and shew hir kind. (*Chronicles*, 6:417)

The stories of the ape in purple velvet and Jupiter's cat reappear 16 pages later to express again the Irish inability to change, when Hooker casts aspersions on the loyalty of the Gaelic-Irish sheriff of Cork, Sir Cormac MacTeige (*Chronicles*, 6:433). Hooker's use of animal imagery, specifically imagery that portrays one returning to one's natural state, no matter how vile, underscores his relentlessly reiterated belief that the Irish were innately vicious and untrustworthy. Though the examples of vomiting dogs and dirt-loving swine demonstrate Hooker's considerable use of simile and metaphor to express filth and corruption, he does not restrict his descriptive vocabulary to animals only. The Renaissance image of the human body as reflective of the commonwealth also appears in such passages as his description of Ireland as "a broken commonweale and ruinous state, being as it were a man altogither infected with sores and biles, and in whose bodie from the crowne of the head to the sole of the foot there is no health" (6:328). Despite his use of such striking visual imagery, Hooker's style can make for tedious reading, especially since he is not particularly interested in the motivation behind the behavior of his historical characters. One's loyalty to the crown is the primary determinant of personal worth. Hooker develops his English protagonists' characters through effusive praise of their ancestry and accomplishments. Conversely, his portrayal of the Irish tends to attacks on character or vituperative commentary on their treasonous nature.

In conclusion, although Hooker's "Supplie" is highly detailed and informative, its style is plodding, lacking Stanyhurst's exuberance and linguistic flair and the delight in anecdote that characterizes Giraldus,

Stanyhurst, and even Holinshed. Hooker does not incorporate direct quotations into the text, preferring to paraphrase speeches and dialogue instead. The overall effect is that of an unrelenting march through a continual series of disasters without the anecdotes, direct quotations, or wry observations that make Stanyhurst so readable. Any analysis that appears in the text is a dreary repetition of the same theme: the wickedness of the Irish, both the Gaelic and those Anglo Irish beyond the Pale, and their lack of appreciation for the many benefits of English civilization. Hooker's antagonism toward Ireland and all things Irish is manifested through his continual harping on the treasonous nature of the Irish and on God's just punishment of them for defying their sovereign. He has nothing but negative observations to make concerning Ireland and its people.

The Irish section of Holinshed's *Chronicles* is noteworthy as a document of both Irish history and English colonialism primarily because the varying experiences and identities of its major contributors create a multivoiced and often contradictory portrayal of Ireland and its inhabitants. The differences between the Irish sections of the 1577 and 1587 *Chronicles* caution us to read the two editions as distinct works that nevertheless inform and define each other. Personal allegiances, national identities, and the vagaries of history have produced a text, that in its very contradictions offers us an inclusive, and therefore perhaps for that reason a more accurate, portrait of colonial Ireland and the English understanding of Irish cultural identity in the sixteenth century. As Annabel Patterson has noted of the Irish contributors in *Reading Holinshed's* Chronicles, "Hooker found himself on the opposite side from Stanyhurst, and the gregarious text of the *Chronicles* faithfully records their differences" (Patterson 1994, 29).

Chapter Five
The "Chronicles of Scotland"

Unlike the "Chronicles of England," compiled by English historians and antiquarians versed in English history, or the "Chronicles of Ireland," which numbered an Anglo-Irish native and English colonizer of Ireland among its writers, none of the contributors to the "Chronicles of Scotland" had ever lived in Scotland or was particularly qualified to write about it. Raphael Holinshed, William Harrison, and Francis Thynne relied primarily on Scottish sources, but their choice of source material raises numerous questions about the ultimate purpose of their respective contributions. Certainly, the "Chronicles of Scotland" was meant to provide a comprehensive history as well as a geographical description of the country, but the authors' privileging of certain sources over others suggests that the "Chronicles of Scotland," particularly the 1577 Scottish history, may have had a particular political agenda as well.

The "Description of Scotland"

Although it heavily relies on Hector Boece's *Scotorum Historiae* (1526), the "Description of Scotland" was obviously supplied by an outsider who had no particular interest in Scotland or any great enthusiasm for the project of describing it. The dedication with which Richard Stanyhurst and William Harrison strove to delineate their respective Irish and English cultures and the beauties and characteristics of their own lands; the pride with which they described their countries' cities, churches, and natural attributes; and the delight in anecdote that characterizes both the "Description of Ireland" and the "Description of England" are sadly lacking in the "Description of Scotland."

The "Description of Scotland" is by far the briefest of the *Chronicles'* descriptions. The text, which Harrison claims to have completed in "three or foure daies," is a loose translation of the geographical information found in the first pages of Hector Boece's *Scotorum Historiae* and John Belenden's abbreviated Scottish translation of Boece's text.[1] In his dedication to Thomas Seckford, Master of Requests and patron of Christopher Saxton's atlas of England and Wales (1579), Harrison admits that he relied primarily on Bellenden's Scottish translation rather than Boece's original Latin text because of his haste to finish the "Description" and because "it is much unfitting for him that professeth Divinite, to applie his time any otherwise unto contemplation of civill histories." This statement does not appear to reflect Harrison's own sentiments, since in chapter 13 of the "Description," he complains, "I will give over not onelie to write more at this present, but for ever hereafter of anie historicall matters, sith I see that this honest kind of recreation is denied me, and all time spent about the same in these daies utterly condemned, as vaine and savouring of negligence, and heathenish impietie" (*Chronicles*, 5:27). Harrison's sensitivity toward critical attacks on clergymen who devote their time to civil histories rather than the mysteries of the divine does not seem to have lasted, as demonstrated by his copious expansion of the 1587 "Description of England."

Although Harrison claims that the looseness of his translation is due to a desire for conciseness, in many sections his text is wordier than the original. Bellenden had divided Boece's Latin work into chapters for his Scottish translation, a format that Harrison follows in the *Chronicles;* however, although Harrison deletes his source's first three chapters on cosmography, he also adds two new chapters to the end of the "Description": a short account of the ancient Picts, based on the Roman authors Herodian and Dion, and a list of Scottish archbishoprics, universities, dukedoms, earldoms, and viscounties.

Despite its comparative brevity, the "Description of Scotland" contains the same elements as the *Chronicles'* English and Irish "Descriptions." The lay of the land and major bodies of water, native population, various cities and towns, natural resources, and local marvels are all discussed, but in an extremely cursory manner. The first chapter lays out Scotland's size, geographical boundaries, and numerous natural resources, which comprise an abundance of livestock, grain, and minerals. The chapter also makes first reference to "the great infirmities that fall unto the people there for their intemperance," a discussion of contemporary Scottish vice that reoccurs throughout the "Description." The second chapter describes the counties, cities, rivers, and lakes of the east, west, and middle borders of Scotland and mentions a few regional distinctions such as the quicksands of the vale of Annand and the cannibalism of the vale's ancient inhabitants. The third chapter includes accounts of Galloway, Kile, Carricke, and Cunningham, while the fourth, fifth, sixth, and seventh chapters similarly deal with other areas of Scotland, listing bodies of water; principal towns, castles, and universities;

and local marvels such as the deaf stone, the great beast of the pool of Argyle, and a stone hollow that renders salt water sweet.

Chapters 8 through 11 of the "Description" consist of information about the native flora and fauna, presenting accounts of both wild and domesticated beasts, including "the strange properties of sundrie Scotish dogs"; a detailed description of the life cycle of the salmon; and curiously extensive discussions of Claike-geese, which supposedly generated out of worms found in driftwood, and Scottish heather, which is described as "verie delicat . . . for goats & all kind of cattell to feed upon, and likewise for diverse foules, but bees especiallie" (*Chronicles*, 5:16). In chapters 12 through 14, significant attention is devoted to the peoples of the Shetland Isles and to the ancient Scots and Picts, all of whom are praised for their simple and virtuous manners of living.

As demonstrated by his continual editorializing, Harrison's authorial presence is pronounced in the first half of the "Description" but disappears almost completely in the final half of the text. In chapters 1 through 7, Harrison deleted most of Boece's and Bellenden's references to supernatural phenomena and Catholic religious traditions, such as shrines to the Virgin and various saints and the practices of Scotland's monasteries and religious houses. For example, Harrison's Scottish source, Bellenden, following Boece, describes how the order of Saint Augustine was regularly sung in the abbey of St. Colme, a passage completely deleted in Harrison. Harrison modified other passages dealing with religious matters or supernatural phenomena with dismissive or derogatory language exhibiting a Protestant's disdain for Catholic piety and an Englishman's condescension for Scottish gullibility. He displays a particular contempt for the veneration of saints' relics. For Bellenden's description of "the Abbey of Quhittern dedicat to the haly bishop sanct Niniane, quahair [where] his blissit [blessed] body restis in gret veration of peple," Harrison substitutes, "an abbie dedicated to saint Ninian the bishop, and there lieth his carcase, which is honored of the people with great superstition and error" (*Chronicles*, 5:4). Bellenden also recounts the existence of a shrine "quhair the blissit banis [bones] of sanct Dutho restis in gret veratioun of peple," a passage that Harrison rewrites as "the bones of Dutho an holy man (as they say) doo rest, & are had in greater estimation among the superstitious sort (as sometime over the whole Iland) than the holie gospell of God and merits of his sonne, whereby we are onelie saved"(5:7).

Harrison also has little patience for accounts of supernatural occurrences or local marvels, topics that fascinated his sources, Boece and Bellenden, both of whom demonstrate a willingness to credit the existence of such phenomena. For example, in his Scottish translation, Bellenden refers to those who believed in the monstrous beast of the pools of Argyle, "which was of the bignesse of a greihound, and footed like a gander," as "sundry prudent men." Bellenden attempts to confirm the animal's authenticity by emphasizing the sound judgment of those who believe in its existence. Harrison, who finds the Argyle story absurd, substitutes, "Those that are given to the observations of rare and uncouth sights" for Bellenden's "sundry prudent men" (*Chronicles*, 5:6). Of the deaf stone, which blocked all sound so completely that a man standing on one side of it could not hear a cannon fired on the other, Harrison sniffs, "[T]o me [it] dooth seeme unpossible" (5:5.) After relating the supposed existence of various other marvels, Harrison finally dismisses the Scots as "verie great observers of uncouth signes & tokens" (5:11).

Harrison's "reformation" of his text by his omitting or rewriting references to what he appears to have considered vain superstition, religious or otherwise, reveals one of the more discreet ways in which the Protestant contributors to Holinshed's *Chronicles* dealt with their primarily Catholic sources. Contributors such as Holinshed, Hooker, and Fleming tended to leave medieval Catholic texts relatively intact while routinely critiquing the content. Instead of providing antipapist anecdotes as did Holinshed, or anti-Catholic commentary in the marginalia and text as did Holinshed, Hooker, and Fleming, Harrison simply deleted or modified textual elements that he found religiously offensive. Harrison's selective adaption of Boece and Bellenden thus refutes the common assumption that the contributors to Holinshed's *Chronicles* failed to exercise discretion in their use of source material. At the same time, Harrison's censoring of material deprives the reader of the interpretive choices available in other sections of the *Chronicles,* most notably in Holinshed's histories. Holinshed presents his material in such a manner that readers are called on to determine the narratives' veracity themselves. Harrison performs this act of interpretation for the reader through deletion and modification of the original information. Harrison obviously assessed his sources with a critical eye but failed to sustain this approach throughout the "Description," as the shift in voice and tone in the last half of the text demonstrates.

This significant shift in voice that occurs in chapters 8 through 13 manifests itself in a variety of ways. The first half of the "Description" alternates between Boece's use of the first-person inclusive "we" to refer

to the Scots and Harrison's third-person reference to "the Scottish men,"
a term that does not appear in his sources. The second half of the
"Description" reverts to a permanently Scottish point of view, signified
by the consistent use of "I" and "we" in its depiction of Scotland's inhabitants and by the disappearance of Harrison's editorializing. The change
in voice appears to be due to Harrison's haste, since his personal commentary also disappears at this point, indicating that he probably
decided it would be quicker merely to translate than to evaluate and
adapt his texts. An example of this change appears in the two descriptions of the Scottish fondness for alcohol in chapters 1 and 13. The evils
of Scottish drunkenness and gluttony depicted in chapter 1 are obviously Harrison's view:

> Therefore it is (as I thinke) that almightie God in his provident dispos-
> tion of all things, hath ordeined their grounds . . . to be destitute and
> void of wine; as foreseeing that the said liquor, which bringeth greatest
> benefit unto other countries, would grow in the end to be most perni-
> cious & noisome to them. For they are given to such unnaturall ravening
> and greedie desire of forreine things (whilst they contemne or not regard
> their owne) that they cannot refraine the immoderate use of wine, and
> excesse used in drinking of the same: insomuch that we may see diverse
> to be overtaken and haunted, not onelie with sundrie kinds of grievous
> maladies common to us and them of the maine, but also manie other
> which they have not. (*Chronicles,* 5:2)

Although the moralistic tone of this passage certainly fits Boece's
continually reiterated theme of the modern Scottish weaknesses of character, its references to the Scottish as "them" and the distinction pointed
out in the phrase "sundrie kindes of grievous maladies common to both
us and *them,*" a line that does not appear in the Latin original or its Scottish translation, marks Harrison's addition. When the same topic is
treated in chapter 13, it is in the words of a Scot admonishing his fellow
countrymen: "But how far we in these present daies are swarved from
the vertes and temperance of our elders, I beleeve there is no man so elo-
quent, nor indued with such utterance, as that he is able sufficientlie to
expresse. For whereas they gave their minds to dowghtinesse, we applie
ourselves to droonkennes: they had plentie with sufficiencie, we have
inordinate excesse with superfluitie: they were temperate, we effemi-
nate: and so is the case now altered with us, that he which can devoure
and drinke most, is the noblest man and most honest companion"
(*Chronicles,* 5:26).

Another indication of Harrison's abdication of authorial voice occurs in the depiction of local piety and supernatural phenomena in the later chapters. Harrison's skeptical asides and textual modifications no longer appear, and the "Description" more closely follows the original narrative. In chapter 10, the miracles that transpire in two chapels dedicated to Saint Peter and Saint Clement on the Isle of Lewis are piously and unquestioningly related: "[T]he fame is, that so soone as the fire goeth out in this Ile, the man that is holden of most cleane and innocent life, goeth to the altar with great solemitie and there laieth a wispe of straw, which being doone they fall all to praier, in the middest whereof fire commeth downe from heaven, and kindleth or setteth the same on fire" (*Chronicles,* 5:17). The miraculous pool of Poinonia, on the Orkney Islands, is depicted in no less credulous a fashion in chapter 12, where its powers to turn wood to iron or stone "farre exceedeth all credit" (5:19). The author then states, "I might (no doubt) have made rehersall of divers other strange things woorthie the noting in this behalfe: but I have made choise onelie of the most rare and excellent" (5:21). Such passages would have been typically deleted or modified by Harrison as in the first half of the "Description," and their inclusion in the original format supports the argument that Harrison was merely translating by this point, since even chapters 14 and 15, which Harrison added to Boece's original work, are devoid of any commentary.

The most significant element of the "Description," the account of Scotland's islanders and ancient inhabitants, evokes classical myths of the golden age and seems designed to provide a moral lesson to the modern Scots rather than an accurate historical portrait. Whereas Boece appears to have incorporated this material into the *Scotorum Historiae* to inspire his countrymen to emulate the habits of their forbears, Harrison's handling of the material in the *Chronicles,* particularly his addition of ancient Roman accounts of the Picts to the end of Boece's narrative, emphasizes the negative attributes of both the ancient and the modern Scots. According to the "Description," only the inhabitants of the Shetland and Outer Islands maintain the ancient Scots' utopian manner of existence: "Certes there is no quarrelling amongst these for wealth or gaine . . . They are void of all ambitious mood, and never troubled with civill or forren warres, as men that deeme firme peace and quietnesse, with mutuall love and amitie, to be the chiefe felicitie to be sought for in this life" (*Chronicles,* 5:20). Like the ancient Scots, the islanders, untainted by foreign decadence, lead vigorous lives of exceptional longevity: "What should I say of their health, which is and may be preferred above all treasure . . . For here among these men, you shall very seldome heare of sickenesse to attach anie, untill extreame age come that killeth them altogither" (5:20). The author's obvious admiration for the simple life of these people forms a striking counterpoint to his rather dim view of the mainland Scots, who "by long sickenesse and languishing greefes doo grow into such deformitie onelie through excessive feeding, and greedie abuse of wine, that if you knew them when they were children & yoong men, you shall hardlie remember them when they be old and aged . . . but rather suppose them to be changelings and monsters" (5:2).

The thirteenth chapter continues this theme by turning to a comparison of the ancient Scots with their descendants. In his depiction of the Spartan dietary habits of the ancient Scots, their simple apparel and frugal manner of life, the author emphasizes their temperance and sobriety, virtues that he claims are in short supply among their progeny. He praises the ancient Scots' military valor, noting that the ancient Scottish women "were of no lesse courage than the men, for all stout maidens & wives (if they were not with child) marched as well in the field as did the men" (*Chronicles*, 5:24). Harrison includes the entire text of Boece's lament over the greed, gluttony, lechery, and drunkenness of his countrymen, whose decline the Scotsman blames on the importation of English manners and morals: "[T]hrough our dailie trades and conversation with them, to learne also their maners, and therwithall their language . . . Heereby shortlie after it came also to passe, that the temperance and vertue of our ancestors grew to be judged worthie of small estimation amongst us" (5:25–26). Harrison refrains from commenting on or criticizing this attack on the English national character, probably because Boece's representation of Scottish national character is far more negative.

Boece's depiction of the Scots' degeneration from their ancestors' nobility of character reveals that Boece had originally designed his *Scotorum Historiae* not merely to record but to inspire, to teach, and to reform. In recounting the virtues of the Scots' ancient forbears, he obviously meant to instill in his contemporaries a spirit of nationalism and a desire to emulate the glories of an idealized past. Harrison's incorporation of Boece's criticism of the Scots into the *Chronicles'* "Description" seems designed for a different purpose, however. When combined with Harrison's depiction of Scottish superstition and gullibility, Boece's moral commentary loses its exhortative thrust, resulting in an exceptionally unflattering portrait of the Scots.

The final two chapters, if they can be called chapters, are Harrison's only original contributions to the "Description." It is unclear why Harrison decided to include a one-page description of the ancient Picts taken from the writings of the ancient Roman historians Herodian and Dion. Its portrayal of the naked, body-painting, violent Picts who held their wives in common, lived in tents, and were "verie readie to steale" is hardly a flattering one and certainly offers a different representation of the ancient inhabitants of Scotland from the one borrowed from Boece in the preceding chapter. Whether Harrison was merely trying to offer a more complete picture of ancient Scotland or whether this chapter is meant as an ironic refutation of Boece's romanticized view of Scotland's past is unclear since Harrison offers no commentary. Other textual evidence, such as Harrison's depiction of Scottish religious superstition and drunkenness and his dismissal of the Scots as credulous fools, as well as his derogatory comments about the ancient Scots in the "Description of England" ("the most Scithian-like and barbarous nation, and longest without letters") would seem to support the latter point of view (*Chronicles*, 1:10). The fifteenth chapter consists solely of a half-page list of archbishoprics, universities, dukedoms, earldoms, and viscounties, without any introduction, explanation, or comment.

Harrison appears to have undertaken the "Description of Scotland" with little enthusiasm, and even the small interest that he expresses at the beginning of the text, as indicated by his interpretation and modification of source material, disappears by chapter 8, where he turns to mere translation of Bellenden and Boece. The result is a text that, although taken from a single source and its translation, is essentially fragmentary, disjointed, and incomplete, offering little information about its subject. Harrison's own prejudices, combined with Boece's point of view, create a strange yet incomplete fusion of an outsider's perception of Scotland and a Scot's understanding of his own country. The unifying thread that holds the text together is the moralizing critique of the contemporary Scots and glorification of their ancestors, a theme that also continues throughout Holinshed's adaption of Boece for the *Chronicles'* Scottish history. In conclusion, Harrison's contribution to the "Chronicles of Scotland" is a hastily assembled and cursory description of Scotland that stands in poor contrast to his "Description of England" or Stanyhurst's "Description of Ireland."

The 1577 "Historie of Scotland"

Holinshed dedicated his history of Scotland to Robert Dudley, earl of Leicester, who at the time of composition was a member of the Privy

Council and master of the queen majesty's horses. Like the 1577 English history, the 1577 Scottish history is divided chronologically by the reigns of kings, each new reign noted by a woodcut depicting a monarch. The same woodcuts employed in the English history appear in the Scottish, again demonstrating that these woodcuts function as a means of visually ordering the text rather than providing a realistic portrait of the monarch. Formulaic woodcuts depicting monarchs interacting with their subjects, courtly festivities, banquets, and processions as well as violent scenes of battles, executions, murders, and other atrocities also occur in both the Scottish and English histories, although some woodcuts, such as those of the Stone at Scone and Macbeth's meeting of the three witches were obviously provided specifically for the Scottish history.[2]

For his account of Scottish history through 1571 Holinshed drew primarily on Boece's *Scotorum Historiae,* and to a lesser extent John Major's *De Gestis Scotorum* (1521). Although Major was a better historian, Boece was the superior storyteller, and his fabulous yarns of early Scottish history, immortalized in Shakespeare's *Macbeth,* must have greatly appealed to Holinshed, whose own penchant for a good anecdote reveals itself throughout his contributions to the *Chronicles.*

At first, Holinshed's privileging of Boece over Major would appear confusing given Boece's often articulated hostility toward the English combined with his strong Scottish nationalism. A stern moralist, Boece often criticizes the luxuriousness and softness of his countrymen, especially in comparison to their hardy and virtuous forbears. He blames English influence and custom, imported during the reign of Malcolm Cammore (1058–1093), for the decline of the Scottish national character. Major, by contrast, expressed a far more conciliatory attitude toward the English and in his writings often articulates his firm belief that Scotland should be united with England.

The fact that Boece had been vociferously discredited in England as a historian well before Holinshed finished compiling his "Chronicles of Scotland" could not have escaped Holinshed's attention, but this also does not seem to have influenced his choice of the Scotsman's text as his chief source of ancient and medieval Scottish history. John Leland, the greatest English antiquarian of the mid–sixteenth century, whose collections formed a significant portion of Reyner Wolfe's manuscripts for the *Chronicles,* had attacked Boece's history, comparing its number of "lies" to "the stars or waves of sea."[3] In 1572, Humfrey Lhuyd, a Welsh antiquarian, described Boece as "a malicious falsifier without all shame or honesty," dismissing Boece's claim that the Scots reigned in Britain three hundred years before Christ's birth, that they were descended from the Egyptians, and that they had any kind of culture or civilization before the coming of the Romans.[4] While Boece still had his admirers, including such well-respected Scottish historians as George Buchanan and Archbishop Spotswoode, even they were uncomfortable with the more grotesque and supernatural aspects of his text, excising or downplaying those elements when they used Boece's history in their own work (Black, 44).

Could Boece's storytelling ability have been the only incentive for Holinshed's wholesale incorporation of the Scottish priest's text into the "Historie of Scotland"? The political events of the 1560s and 1570s suggest that other reasons may have also been at issue. Boece's history argues that the Scottish monarchy was the most ancient in Europe and describes how from its very beginnings the Scottish monarchy was accountable to its people. This last point, illustrated through the reigns of Boece's 45 kings, demonstrates that a relationship of mutual rights and obligations between ruler and subject had been the operative principle of Scottish government for almost seven hundred years, between the reigns of Fergus I (ca. 330 B.C.) and Fergus II (360 A.D.). Those kings who terrorized their subjects or used their power for their own selfish appetites were either driven into exile, put to death, or imprisoned, sometimes even committing suicide to escape punishment for their wicked deeds. Through the precedent set by the example of his ancient kings, Boece argued that the Scottish people had the right to withdraw sovereign power from a monarch who failed to live up to the trust vested in him. Though medieval political theory may have argued that unjust and tyrannical rulers may be lawfully deposed from power, no one had ever suggested that the history of an entire country had operated on such a principle.

Despite small details such as that until Boece, no one had ever heard or read of these 45 kings, let alone the sources that Boece claimed to have found to support their existence, his history exerted a significant influence on Scotland's troubled politics later in the century, playing a role in the deposition of Mary, Queen of Scots, in 1567. When Queen Elizabeth sent Sir Nicholas Throckmorton to the Scottish nobles to account for the capture and imprisonment of their sovereign, they quoted Boece's historical precedents as a justification for their action. Throckmorton, citing the untouchable sovereignty of kings and accusing the nobles of treason, was answered with the argument "that in extraordinary enormities and monstrous doings . . . the states of the realm, and the people assembled, might in the case be competent judges, whereof they had in their own country sundry experiences in criminal matters committed by princes; and there was recited unto me sundry examples forth out of their own histories" (Black, 39). George Buchanan, whose own *Rerum Scoticarum Historia* (1582) was one of the primary sources for Francis Thynne's update and expansion of the 1587 "Chronicles of Scotland," also used Boece to justify to the rest of Europe the act of deposition in his *De Jure apud Scotos* (1579).

Boece's *Scotorum Historiae* would have also served a particular English political agenda at this point in history. When Mary fled her Scottish prison of Lochleven for England in 1568, she had hoped for Elizabeth's assistance in her restoration to the Scottish throne. Elizabeth, despite her horror at the Scottish rebellion, for political purposes chose to allow Mary's half-brother, the earl of Moray, to continue as regent for the infant James VI. Mary remained in England, a prisoner for the next 18 years and the focal point of numerous Catholic plots, both real and imagined, to raise her to the English throne. Despite the Northern Rebellion of 1569, which sought to free Mary and secure her succession to the English Crown, and the Ridolfi plot of 1572, which sought to depose Elizabeth and enthrone Mary, Elizabeth, ignoring the urges of her Privy Council, refused to take any action against her cousin. As early as 1572, the Bishop of London had called for the Scottish queen's execution, but not until the Babington plot of 1585 revealed that Mary had approved of Elizabeth's assassination did the English queen reluctantly, and under tremendous pressure from the Privy Council and Parliament, sign the warrant for Mary's death. Her reason for procrastinating was that "absolute princes ought not to be accountable for their actions to any other than to God alone" (Guy, 278, 335–336).

It would be impossible to prove that Holinshed's circulation of a chronicle history that clearly depicted Scottish monarchs as accountable to others besides God for their actions affected English popular opinion regarding Mary's execution, or had any influence on the Privy Council or Parliament. Yet it certainly can be said that Holinshed's "Historie of Scotland" offered a justification for such an action to a wide English audience, certainly a wider audience than either Boece's Latin text or Bellenden's Scottish translation had reached. The "Historie of Scotland" provided a solution to the "Mary problem" without ever mentioning the queen within the context of Boece's 45 kings. It is also possible that Holinshed's incorporation of Boece into his history served as an apology for England's position on Mary's deposition by demonstrating that her loss of the throne was the result not of English intervention but Scottish politics, based on historical precedence. Boece's *Scotorum Historiae* was the only Scottish history in existence at that time that could have furnished Holinshed with material claiming Scottish historical precedence for the deposition and execution of an unworthy monarch. Furthermore, the depiction of a people's right to depose a monarch within the "safe" context of foreign custom provided Holinshed with an arena in which to explore such sensitive topics as the nature of rule and the obligations of a ruler to his people.

Holinshed's account of the Scots' origin in ancient Greece and Egypt about 1500 B.C.; their travels through the Mediterranean; and their founding of a new kingdom in Spain, a colony in Ireland, and finally the Scottish colony of Dalriada (Argyll) in the fifth century B.C. can be found in Boece as well as in the work of the fourteenth-century historian John of Fordun and the other medieval Scottish chroniclers whom Holinshed also consulted for his history. Until Boece's *Scotorum Historiae* appeared in 1526, however, no record of any Scottish king's reign between the fourth century B.C. and the fourth century A.D. existed, although John of Fordun claimed that 45 kings had ruled during this time.

In the *Scotorum Historiae,* Boece provided not only the names of the 45 kings but also a detailed account of each of their reigns. The most striking elements of that section of Holinshed's Scottish history based on Boece are the Scots' complete intolerance of evil or corrupt rulers, and the Scottish queens' methods of dealing with unfaithful husbands. The wives of Maldwin and Fergus III strangle their husbands in their beds for keeping concubines, and Brenna strangles her second husband, the Pictish king Enganus, in revenge for treacherously killing her first husband, his brother (*Chronicles*, 5:177, 183, 194). According to the Scottish history, the early Scots held their monarch accountable for his personal as well as political deeds, and Scottish kings were deposed and murdered for their unruly physical appetites as often as for their inability to rule well. King Durstus, given to "banketting and excessive drunkenesse" and the despoiler of his peers' "substance and inheritence," is murdered by his indignant subjects (5:52–53) The wicked and lecherous Ewin is cast into prison and later murdered there. Lugthake, "abhorred of all men for his detestable and filthie vices, joined with all kinds of crueltie and covetousnesse," is killed in assembly by a crowd that includes his own bodyguards (5:86). Mogall, who starts his rule well and is beloved by his subjects, ultimately degenerates into a greedy lecher and murderer of his nobles. Finally, his head is cut off, set on the end of a pole, and derisively carried aloft in a manner strikingly similar to that of a later and more infamous Scottish king, Macbeth. Conversely, the text celebrates kings such as Gregory, Malcolm, and David for their sexual chastity, sobriety, and godliness. This peculiar emphasis on personal rather than political virtue can again be attributed to Holinshed's reliance on the moralist Boece, who had designed his *Scotorum Historiae* as a "mirror for princes."

Holinshed does not present Scotland's long and bloody history of regicides entirely without comment. Whether out of personal discomfort or to circumvent official disapproval, he occasionally makes notes in the margins such as "Regicides or kingquellers ought chieflie above all other to be punished," and he perfunctorily dismisses the assassination of vicious kings as "wicked deeds." At the same time, he carefully includes all of Boece's references to the numerous vices and outrages committed by these kings as well as the well-merited indignation of their subjects. The pattern established with Boece's 45 kings continues to inform the narrative of later kings' reigns in that the accountability of Scottish monarchs to their people does not appear only during the seven hundred years between the two Ferguses' reigns but continues into the period of later monarchs as well, as we see in Boece's extensive history of Macbeth. Boece's account of Macbeth's reign is one of the longest and most detailed in the text. To Boece's lively imagination, as passed down through Holinshed's history, Shakespeare owes the account of the weird sisters' appearance and prophecies; Lady Macbeth's ambition; Macbeth's guilty conscience and decision to kill Banquho and Fleance; Malcolm's test of Macduff by depicting himself as lustful and avaricious (the traditional vices of bad Scottish kings); and the death of Macbeth at the hands of the avenger Macduff, "not of woman born." At the same time, Shakespeare deletes the numerous elements of Macbeth's story that depict his reign as typical of Scotland's history to underscore the depravity into which the Scottish king's character descends. For example, both Duncan and Macbeth, as first cousins, have a claim to the Scottish throne through their mothers' line. Duncan, a weak and incompetent ruler, is executed by a number of his nobles, including Macbeth and Banquho, because of their dissatisfaction with his rule. In the Scottish history, Duncan is merely another example of a monarch punished for his failure to rule well. Macbeth, like other Scottish kings before him, begins his reign auspiciously, the "most diligent punisher of all injuries and wrongs attempted by anie disordered persons within his realme, [he] was accounted the sure defense and buckler of innocent people; and hereto he also applied his whole indevor, to cause yoong men to exercise themselves in vertuous maners, and men of the church to attend their divine service according to their vocations" (*Chronicles*, 5:270). His fear of being deposed by one of his own nobles—a common enough occurrence, as the Scottish history demonstrates—leads to his bloody reign of terror, and his assassination, like that of Duncan before him, is the typical Scottish response to a bad king. In the Scottish history, Macbeth is simply part of a pattern rather than an exceptional villain.

Along with the monarch's accountability to his people, the informing motif of the Scottish history is the question of the Scottish succession. The Scottish history attributes the problems of Scottish succession to the tradition of choosing a king by vote when there is no heir of sufficient age, a practice that the Scots claimed went back to the reign of Fergus I in the fourth century B.C. and was finally abolished centuries later during the reign of Kenneth II (971–995 A.D.): "This ordinance also they decreed to be observed as a law from thencefoorth ever after, that if the king died leaving no issue, but such as were under age to succeed him, then should one of his neerest coosins, such as was thought meetest to occupie the roome, be chosen to reigne as king during his life, and after his deceasse the crowne to revert unto his predecessors issue without controversie, if the same were once growne up to lawfull age" (*Chronicles*, 5:43–44). As the text notes, though such a custom avoids the dangers that accompany a child ruler, it was rare for the crown to revert back to its original owners without a bloody squabble. Thus the Scottish history depicts a notable number of uncles who murder their nephews and nephews who slaughter their uncles and cousins in their attempts to seize the throne. From its inception, the practice was surrounded by suspected treachery and violence. Feritharis, brother of Fergus I and the first to be crowned under this law, "lived not passing three moneths after this businesse, but died suddenlie in the night, the truth not being knowne whether by naturall death, or through treason" (5:44). Caught between its traditions of royal succession and of royal accountability, ancient Scotland is characterized by a cycle of kings deposed, assassinated for their own tyranny, or murdered through their kinsmen's treachery. Rarely does a Scottish monarch die peacefully in his own bed.

From Boece also, Holinshed draws numerous accounts of bizarre and supernatural phenomena, although this is by no means unique to the Scottish history. If there is one element common to all portions of Holin-

shed's *Chronicles,* it is this fascination with supernatural events, which fill
the pages of the histories and descriptions alike. As in the other *Chronicles* histories, these events usually portend some disastrous occurrence.
For example, the Roman conquest of the Scots is foreshadowed by fiery
visions in the air, a downpour of frogs, and the birth of a hermaphrodite.
The Danish invasion is heralded by the appearance of the Bassinates,
"fishes in great numbers, like unto men in shape, swimming up and
downe in the streame with halfe their bodies above the water, and having a blacke skin, which covered their heads and necks, from their
shoulders upwards like an hood." Their appearance signified "some
great misfortune unto the countrie, as the common people have long
had an opinion" (*Chronicles*, 5:216–17). The reign of James I (who was
killed by assassins) is characterized by "sundrie strange and monstrous
things" such as a sow that gave birth to a litter of pigs with heads like
dogs, a cow that gave birth to a calf with the head of a horse, and a
sword that moved through the air "to the no lesse dread than woonder
of the people" (5:428). There is a marked drop in such descriptions once
other authors replace Boece as the primary narrative source. In fact,
compared to the English history, the later fifteenth and sixteenth centuries of the Scottish history are remarkably lacking in tales of the
bizarre and supernatural.

Whereas Holinshed uses Boece as a source until the death of James I
in 1461, from 875 on Holinshed employs John Major's *Historia Majoris
Britanniae tam Angliae Quam Scotiae* (1521) with increasing frequency.
Beginning with the reign of Robert Bruce (1306–1328), John Major
supersedes Boece as Holinshed's primary source and continues as such
into the early sixteenth century. Because of its reliance on Major, who,
unlike Boece, approached historical legends with a highly critical eye,
this portion of Holinshed's text is markedly less flamboyant in its depiction of Scottish history, although it is no less full of violent upheaval and
rebellion. From the dispute between Robert Bruce and John Baliol over
their respective claims to the Scottish throne through the death of
James III in 1488, the Scottish history continues its bloody cycle. One of
its more noteworthy developments is the growing entanglement of
Scottish and English history. The earlier history of Scottish-English relations depicts a tedious series of interminable border skirmishes between
the two countries; however, beginning with Edward I's claims of
suzerainty over Scotland at the end of the thirteenth century and continuing through the reign of Elizabeth I, Scottish and English politics
become more closely entwined as the "Historie of Scotland" continues,

and the perspective gradually shifts from a Scottish to an English point of view, especially as Holinshed becomes more dependent on the English chroniclers listed in his sources at the beginning of the history. This is especially true of the sixteenth-century Scottish history, which is drawn almost solely from English sources.

England's attempt to force a betrothal between Edward VI and Mary, Queen of Scots, is depicted as a sincere desire for friendship and accord, and Henry VIII's attempts to achieve control over Scotland is downplayed by the history's portrayal of him as a loving uncle expressing concern for his nephew James V. Although only Edward Hall is mentioned in the marginalia, from the late fifteenth century through the end of 1577 Holinshed appears to have relied primarily on Hall, Richard Grafton, and John Stow for his information, since none of his Scottish sources provided histories for this later period. Boece's history ends in 1436 and Major's text, a slender volume that included the history of England as well as of Scotland, ends with Henry VIII's marriage to Catherine of Aragon.

Despite its reliance on English sources, Holinshed's treatment of Mary of Guise and Mary, Queen of Scots, in the Scottish history is typically objective and even-handed. As is the case in the English history, the more recent the events, the less commentary Holinshed offers concerning them. He refrains from any partisan religious or political commentary, reporting on the two queens' lives in a straightforward, factual manner. His concluding remarks concerning the French Catholic Mary of Guise are even complimentary, blaming the troubles of her regency on the advice of bad councillors rather than on any weaknesses of hers: "She was a wise and verie prudent princesse, and in hir time had learned good experience of the nature and inclination of the nobilitie and people of Scotland. During the time that she was regent, she kept good justice, and was well obeied in all parts of the realme in Orkeneie, and the westerne Isles. And if she had to hir owne experience joined the councell of the nobles and wise men of the realme of Scotland, without following the advise of strangers, there had beene never question nor debate betweixt her and the nobilitie, as some deemed" (*Chronicles*, 5:603).

Although Holinshed thoroughly depicts the myriad troubles of the early reign of Mary, Queen of Scots, he lets events speak for themselves. For example, his account of the scandal surrounding the death of Mary's second husband, Darnley, and her subsequent hasty marriage to his suspected assassin, Bothwell, is notable for its laconic brevity, especially in comparison to the extensive detail supplied by Thynne in the 1587 edition of the *Chronicles*. Whereas Thynne provides a substantial narrative of the entire affair, including Bothwell's supposed abduction of Mary, the political uproar over their relationship, the queen's defense of her marriage to her husband's suspected assassin, and Bothwell's miserable end in a Danish prison, Holinshed merely states that although Bothwell was suspected of the murder, he was acquitted and married the queen, and that some of the Scottish nobility raised arms and attacked Bothwell and the queen at Bockwicke Castle. Yet even without commentary, Holinshed's depiction of Mary's life, when placed within the larger context of the Scottish history, evokes the memory of Boece's ancient Scottish kings whose failure to rule well resulted in the loss of their thrones and often the loss of their lives.

Although the closing pages of the Scottish history do have a pronounced English point of view, Holinshed manages to offer some uniquely Scottish perceptions of English history throughout the "Historie of Scotland," drawn, of course, from his Scottish sources. From Boece, he borrows the account of the legendary King Arthur's final battle with his nephew Mordred. According to the Scots, Arthur is the villain who treacherously rescinded Mordred's legitimate claim to the English throne (*Chronicles*, 5:159–60). From John Major, Holinshed appropriates the Scottish legend of how Richard II of England was not executed but escaped from prison in feminine disguise and entered into service with a Scotsman named MacDonald. According to this account, when his true identity was discovered, he was taken to King Robert and royally entertained. Richard later entered a life of contemplation, died, and was buried in a Blackfriars monastery (5:403). The Scottish histories, unlike those of the English, support the legitimacy of Perkin Warbeck's claim to be Richard, duke of York, although the *Chronicles'* version amply documents James IV's growing disillusionment with the pretender (5:463). Perhaps the most poignant example of Scottish revisionism involves the disastrous defeat and death of James IV and his forces in their battle with the English at Flodden Field in 1513: "Manie thought it was not the body of King James which the Englishmen found in the field, and tooke it for his; but rather an other Scotish mans corps, called the lard of Bonehard, who was also slaine there. And it was affirmed by sundrie, that the king was seene the same night alive at Kelso: and so it was commonlie thought that he was living long after, and that he passed the seas into other countries, namelie to Jerusalem to visit the holie Sepulchre, and so to drive foorth the residue of his daies, in doing penance for his former passed offenses: but he appeared not in

Scotland after as king" (5:482). Whether consciously or not, the Scottish version of the monarch's final days is eerily reminiscent of Celtic legends depicting the hero's passage into the other world and of the Arthurian legend of Perceval's last days in Jerusalem. James IV's earlier attempts to organize Christian Europe into a new Crusade against the Turks had failed, yet Scottish tradition granted the idealistic monarch his long-desired vision of the Holy Land.

Though he may have included some of the more fantastic claims of Scottish history, Holinshed did not approach his sources naively, and indeed, he is most critical of his major source, Boece. Holinshed did not seek to write the definitive Scottish history so much as to make accessible all available Scottish histories. Through his commentary on his sources, he demonstrates that he thoroughly comprehends their lack of veracity, but more importantly he understands their function not necessarily as histories, but as political propaganda. In defense of the more preposterous elements that he includes from these narratives, he states, "But this discourse have I made according to their owne histories, least I should seeme to defraud them of whatsoever glorie is to be gotten by errours, as the maner is of them as well as of other nations, which to advance their antiquities and glorie of their ancestors, take the advantage oftentimes of writers scant woorthie of credit" (*Chronicles*, 5:62).

The text and marginalia of the "Historie of Scotland" are filled with skeptical asides and critical comments aimed at the integrity of the Scottish historians. Holinshed scoffs at their accounts of the Scots' origin and questions their dating of the Scots' arrival in the British Isles. He discredits their accounts of Richard II and James IV as "vaine opinion." He corrects Boece's account of the Scottish resistance to the Romans' invasion, stating that while he may have followed Boece's history closely, he did so clearly recognizing the dubious nature of many of his assertions and assuming that his readers would do the same: "And for that we meane not to presume wholie to derogat the same Boetius [Boece] his credit, we have not much dissented from him, but rather followed him in most places, leaving such doubts as may be woorthilie put foorth of that which he writeth, unto the consideration of the diligent reader, sith it is not our purpose to impugne, but rather to report what we find written by others, except now and then by the way to admonish the reader of some unlikeliehoods (as the same dooth seeme to us and others) and happily not without just occasion" (*Chronicles*, 5:193).

This passage clearly and concisely articulates Holinshed's historical methodology not only in the Scottish history, but in the English and

Irish histories as well. He presents readers with a multitude of available sources, letting readers decide which sources can be trusted and which cannot but simultaneously guiding them with interpretative signposts to lead them to conclusions that do not reproduce the political views, superstitions, or religious errors that he appears to find so offensive in his sources. Although Holinshed created a multivocal narrative through his combining of numerous and often contradictory sources, as Annabel Patterson has admirably demonstrated, he did not entirely leave the text open to any and all interpretations (Patterson 1994, 40–42).

The 1587 "Historie of Scotland"

The 1587 edition of the "Chronicles of Scotland" retains the underlying structure of the original, including Harrison's "Description," Holinshed's history, and Holinshed's dedicatory epistle to Leicester. The order is changed slightly, with the dedication appearing before the Scottish history and immediately after the "Description" instead of at the beginning of the entire Scottish section, as it does in the 1577 edition. Although the 1587 "Description" contains minor editorial changes, the content remains unchanged. Francis Thynne, who provided the 1587 continuation and expansion of the "Historie of Scotland," added substantial information to the history from the thirteenth century on, extended the narrative from 1571 to 1586, and appended an annotated list of Scottish authors apparently modeled on Stanyhurst's list of authors found at the end of the 1577 Irish history.

There is virtually no difference between the earliest sections of the 1577 and the 1587 historical narratives except for minor editorial changes such as the use of Gothic instead of italic print for the marginalia; an occasional deletion or addition of a marginal note; minor spelling variations; and the setting off of speeches and other significant passages through quotations, subheadings, or larger type in the 1587 edition. The differences between the 1577 and the 1587 texts become increasingly marked from the year 1292 on as Thynne's contributions to the existing Scottish history become more numerous and expansive. Drawn primarily from George Buchanan's *Rerum Scoticarum Historia* (1582) and John Leslie's *De Origine, Moribus, et Rebus Gestis Scotorum* (1578), these additions clarify certain details and develop existing information. Unlike the additions to the 1587 English history, which are often tangential, these passages are well incorporated into the text and significantly improve rather than detract from the narrative. Thynne's additions are carefully marked in the margins with Thynne's name or initials and citations of sources.

One of the more curious elements of the 1587 "Historie of Scotland" is the appearance of Thynne's primary sources, Buchanan and Leslie, as historical actors in his text. Buchanan, a Protestant who later became tutor to James VI, is portrayed escaping religious persecution during James V's reign: "In this yeare . . . were manie taken for Lutheranisme, whereof some were burnt; nine recanted, and manie banished: amongst whom George Buchanan was one, who escaped by a rope of a window of a chamber" (*Chronicles*, 5:515). John Ross, bishop of Ross, appears as a powerful clergyman and trusted advisor to Mary, Queen of Scots, and later as an influential Catholic exile in Lyons, France (5:690).

In the Scottish history, Thynne refrains from analyzing cause and motive and restricts himself to reporting events. Thynne articulates his desire to avoid any appearance of partisanship, especially religious partisanship, noting that "my pen and purpose is bent to treat of politicall and not spirituall causes" (*Chronicles* 5:706). Strangely enough, in his attempts to present the events of the Scottish Reformation in as objective a light as possible, Thynne often relied more heavily on the work of the Catholic Ross than on that of the Protestant Buchanan. His narrative of Cardinal David Beaton's assassination, taken from Leslie's *De Origine,* is a particularly interesting example of Thynne's historical method concerning matters of religion, given that Beaton, who was responsible for the death of the Protestant martyr George Wishart, was extremely unpopular among Protestants. Although John Knox had described Beaton's death as a just revenge for "the shedding of the blood of that notable instrument of God, Master George Whishart" and referred to Beaton as "an obstinate enemy against Jesus Christ," Thynne follows Leslie in condemning the murder as "a wicked and shameful deed" (5:546).[5] Thynne's attempts to achieve a balanced presentation of religious issues also occurs in his discussion of Mary's arrival in 1561 to take over the government of Scotland and of the ensuing religious tension. He begins his account with reference to an act made by the lords of the council declaring that Scotland would remain Protestant under Mary's rule, although the Catholic queen and her family would be permitted to hear Mass privately. He then relates how during the preparation for one such private Mass on the first Sunday after her arrival, "[O]ne of the companie snatched awaie the wax candels and brake them: by occasion whereof (if some of the houshold had not come betweene to helpe in that action, and ended the same) all the other fur-

niture had beene throwne downe." Thynne continues with a report of
the various public reactions to the resulting riot, without privileging one
view over any other: "[S]ome blaming it as a most sawcie part; other
interpreting it, that it was onelie doone to trie the patience of the priest;
and some judged and said that the priest was woorthie to be punished
with that paine which the scripture appointeth to idolaters" (5:609).
Thynne draws on both Leslie and Buchanan for his account of the events
surrounding the incident, and his treatment of the affair again demonstrates his effort to be as nonpartisan as possible.

Although Thynne made every effort to remain objective in his depiction of the more recent events of Scottish history, his attitude toward his
Scottish sources reveals little of that same equanimity. Like Holinshed,
Thynne is highly dismissive of the Scottish historians. He often dispar-
ages their claims, implying that they are lying, particularly in the
reports of English and Scottish relations. Nevertheless, compared to the
1587 histories of Ireland and England, the 1587 Scottish history is far
less polarized in its portrayal of historical events, even when Thynne's
occasional snipes at the Scottish historians are taken into account.

Attacks on Scottish historians first appear in Thynne's additions to
the medieval section of the Scottish history. Thynne ridicules such Scottish national heroes as Robert Bruce and William Wallace by scornfully
dismissing the claims of the Scottish historians who recorded their
deeds. Referring to John Major's depiction of Robert Bruce embracing
the members of his army before battle, Thynne notes that "the king
came downe the hill, on which he stood, when he uttered these woords,
and bareheaded imbraced all the nobilitie in his armes, and after turning
himselfe to the whole armie, he reached to everie man his hand in signe
of amite: but I suppose he was overwearied before he had shaken 35,000
men by the hands"(*Chronicles,* 5:346). Thynne concludes the narrative of
William Wallace's life with the note that even the Scottish historian
John Major found Scottish praise of Wallace hard to believe: "Of this
William Wallase one Henrie, who was blind from his birth, in the time
of my nativitie (saith John Major) composed a whole booke in vulgar
verse, in which he mitred all those things vulgarlie spoken of this Wallase. But I doo not in all points, saith the same author, give credit to the
writings of such as he was, who onelie get their food and clothing . . . by
reciting of histories before the nobilite of Scotland" (5:339). The singling out of Bruce and Wallace certainly appears to be based on their
roles in Scotland's national resistance against English rule since Thynne
does not level such dismissive attacks on their contemporary, the En-

glish sympathizer John Balliol. In fact, when the Scottish nobility are
portrayed in the text as dismayed by Balliol's pledge of homage to
Edward I, Thynne implies that the nobility favored English sovereignty
in Scotland with his marginal note, "So say the Scotish writers, but how
trulie, read more heerof in England" (5:30).

Thynne's sharpest attacks are aimed at one of his primary sources,
George Buchanan. He may have borrowed heavily from Buchanan's
Rerum Scoticarum Historia, but he often writes of the Scottish historian
with real hostility, primarily because of Buchanan's numerous and
pointed attacks on such English and Welsh historians as Hall, Grafton,
and Lhuyd in his own works: "Buchanan, whose name may rightlie be
deduced from "Bucca vana," beyond all modestie and course of reason
forgetting his calling, his learning and humanitie, hath spued out all his
malice against the English nation, whereof I have treated in my former
additions to the historie of Scotland" (*Chronicles,* 5:695). In an interesting turn of events, Thynne condemns Buchanan for ridiculing the
Britons' claim to be descended from Brutus and for stating that "he can
rather proove the Britians to be made of dogs and brute beasts." Thynne
also defends Humfrey Lhuyd's dismissal of Hector Boece's history as
untrue and criticizes Buchanan's attack on Lhuyd for questioning Boece:
"And is this so great a fault in Lhoid, when himselfe [Buchanan] and
Lesleus bishop of Rosse (secretlie misliking Boetius) have in silence
passed over a great manie imperfections in the historie of Boetius, and
placed manie other things after an other sort, referring them to other
times than Boetius dooth? And why should he maligne Lhoid for repre-
hending him, whome himself condemneth?" (5:415–16) Thynne's diatribe against Buchanan reveals that the *Chronicles'* multivocality comes
not only from its inclusion of multiple and sometimes contradictory
sources, but also from the continuing dialogue between the *Chronicles*
and its source material. Ironically, Thynne attacks Buchanan for raising
the same issues concerning the historical veracity of the English chronicles that Holinshed and he have raised concerning their own Scottish
sources. Furthermore, Thynne finds himself in the position of defending
such legendary claims of English history as the Britons' descent from
Brutus, while at the same time continuing to question similar claims in
Scottish history. In this particular example, a fascinating discourse concerning the issue of historical veracity is shaped by the interplay of
voices found in Holinshed's commentary on the 1577 Scottish history's
primary sources (Boece and Major), overlaid by Thynne's commentary
on the 1587 Scottish history's primary sources (Buchanan and Leslie).

In addition to his expansion of the existing Scottish history, Thynne provided the 1587 Scottish chronicles with the "Continuation of the Annales of Scotland," an update of Scottish events from 1571 to 1586. The "Continuation" is dedicated to the reader, for unlike his fellow contributors, Thynne did not dedicate any of his work in the *Chronicles* to an individual patron. In the "Continuation," Thynne continues to rely on Buchanan and Leslie for material, but because both these sources end their histories well before 1586, he had to fashion his later history out of what he could put together himself:

> I omit manie things in this my continuance of the Annales of Scotland, & have reported things in other formes than some mens humors would have had me to doo: I must desire thee to consider for the first that the Scots themselves, beside manie others of our owne nation are the cause thereof, who either for feare durst not, or for pretended advise and consultation in the matter would not, or for the restreint of others might not, impart to me such things as should both concerne the honour of the Scotish nation, and the substance of their owne cause." (*Chronicles*, 5:656)

Thynne often complains of his difficulty in acquiring promised material, and it is obvious that he struggled to develop his history to a respectable length. The narrative is fragmented and poorly organized, wandering freely from topic to topic. Thynne fills out his work with reprints of official proclamations and declarations and incorporates a number of digressions that only tangentially relate to the text's history. In fact, most of the "Continuation" consists of Thynne's interminable catalogues reminiscent of those that he provided for the 1587 English history. These include "The protectors, governours, or regents of Scotland, during the king's minoritie or his insufficiency of government, or during his absence out of the realme"; an explanation of the origin of the office of chancellor with an etymology of the term; the military exploits of the Scots in the Low Countries; catalogues of the dukes of Scotland and those Scots that had become dukes elsewhere; a catalogue of the archbishops of Saint Andrew; and "a general catalogue of all the writers in Scotland, with the times in which they lived." Indeed, after the expurgations and reformations executed upon Thynne's "Continuation" during the censorship of the *Chronicles,* the narrative was left with very little historical information at all.

Thynne continues to avoid any appearance of religious bias in the "Continuation," although his sympathies clearly lie with the "king's faction," who were Protestants and supporters of an English alliance, as opposed to the "queen's faction," who were backed by the French and the Roman Catholic Church. Yet even when presenting a Protestant viewpoint, Thynne makes an effort to maintain the semblance of objective reporting by crediting the religious perspective to his sources, not his own beliefs. For example, after his notably sympathetic account of the Protestant earl of Morton's conduct during the earl's examination and execution in 1581, Thynne offers what appears to be a disclaimer for his positive portrait of Morton: "Thus far the confession and death of the earle Morton, penned by such of the presbyterie as were present thereat, and favored him in all respects, seeking to cleere him of anie evill imposed against him. In setting downe whereof, I have not varied from the verie words of my copie in manner of penning it" (*Chronicles*, 5:704–5). Despite his Protestant sympathies, Thynne's 1587 portrayal of the Reformation in Scotland lacks the partisan histrionics so apparent in Fleming's 1587 depiction of the same event in England, and his impartial report of that tumultuous time depicts both Catholics and Protestants with equal sympathy and dignity.

The "Continuation" depicts Scotland in a continual state of political chaos. The narrative focuses on Mary's unpopularity, James's youth and inexperience, and the constant quarreling and jockeying for power among the nobles. Although the "Continuation" appeared barely a month before the execution of Mary, Queen of Scots, on 8 February 1587, no real mention is made of the Babington plot or any of the events leading up to her execution, even to cross-reference these events to their full-blown depiction in the English history, the usual procedure in the *Chronicles* when events in the Scottish or Irish history are more fully treated in the "Chronicles of England." Like Holinshed, Thynne becomes more reticent and discreet in his writing as he approaches more recent events, and he may have felt that the Babington plot was too politically dangerous to treat in any detail. Despite his caution, the "Continuation" was significantly censored in 1587.

Although Thynne's additions and expansions to the original 1577 text remained untouched by censorship, his "Continuation" was significantly revised. The principal foci of censorship are those passages dealing with English intervention in Scottish domestic affairs and those depicting Scotland's civil disorder and court corruption during James VI's reign, or, in the words of the Privy Council when it ordered a halt to the sale and distribution of the *Chronicles*, "[S]uch mention of matter touching the King of Scottes as may give him cause for offense" (*APC*, xiv:311–12).

The first excision involves events of 1578, including a discussion of the chancellors of Scotland, the military actions of the Scots in the Low Countries, and English military raids into Scotland against members of Lennox's party during the factional strife between Lennox and Morton. Though much of the material seems an unlikely target for censorship, the English military raids do contradict English claims of noninvolvement in Scottish affairs, and Thynne specifically links the civil unrest in Scotland during this period to King James's ineffective rule: "But leaving the Scots rejoising of this good successe in those low countries, we will call backe our pen and resalute the countrie of Scotland, at this time in some civill dissentions amongst themselves, whereof these manie yeares since the government of this yoong king, it seemeth to me that it hath not long beene free" (*Chronicles*, 5:688).

The second point of excision depicts Thomas Randolph's appointment as ambassador to Scotland after Morton's death, reports of James Stewart's unethical machinations to secure the title of earl of Arran, the exchange of ambassadors between France and Scotland, and the detention of the Scottish Jesuit William Creighton for plotting against the queen. As Cyndia Clegg has noted, James Stewart had been one of King James's favorites, and references to his coup against the English-supported Morton and his acquisition of the earldom by persuading "the lunatike earle of Arrane, a grant and departure of his right and title, and honor to the earledome of Arrane" would probably have not pleased James (Clegg 1997, 154–56). England's arrest and questioning of William Creighton would possibly have supplied more embarrassing evidence of English involvement in Scottish domestic affairs because Creighton was a vocal supporter of D'Aubigny's claim to the Scottish throne as a means of achieving Catholic control of Scotland. The *Chronicles'* account of how Creighton cooperated with Walsingham in providing evidence about William Parry in exchange for his own liberty again points to England's taking an active role in Scottish affairs despite claims to the contrary.

The last passage to be censored concerns the breakdown in diplomatic relations between England and Scotland from 1584 through 1586. It begins with the failed efforts of the Scottish ambassador, Louis Bellenden, to have the earls of Angus and Mar returned to Scotland to stand trial for their role in a failed plot to overthrow James Stewart, earl of Arran. A year later, Elizabeth demanded the surrender of the earl of Arran for his role in the death of the English Lord Russell during a border dispute. When James VI refused to comply, she sent Angus and Mar back to Scotland in October 1585. The "Banished Lords" raised an army, took possession of the young king, and had Arran proclaimed a traitor. A "League of Friendship" was finally formed between England and Scotland in 1586 in which Elizabeth granted James a pension in exchange for his pledge to give no aid to Elizabeth's enemies and to assist her with troops if England was attacked. Also touching on Scottish-English relations in this section is an account of the transfer of custody of Mary, Queen of Scots, from the earl of Shrewsbury to Sir Ralph Sadler and then to Sir Amie Paulet. The expurgated text deletes most of the details of these tumultuous years, supplying instead King James's speech to the Scottish Parliament concerning the league with England and the proclamation issued by the "Banished Lords" on their return to Scotland, with only brief general paragraphs to link the two.

As both Anne Castanien and Cyndia Clegg have argued, the censorship of the "Historie of Scotland" focuses on those events potentially offensive to James VI, including Scotland's chronic political instability and England's direct intervention in Scotland's domestic affairs, which James was known to strongly oppose. Although Thynne's account of this period of Scottish history is objectively narrated and devoid of inflammatory political commentary, the circumstances speak for themselves. The original text presented a Scotland torn by civil dissension and governed by a young and inexperienced king incapable of managing his affairs without outside intervention. The expurgated text suppresses this unflattering portrait of James and minimizes England's role in his early reign (Castanien, 201–24; Clegg 1997, 153–56).

Despite the efforts of the Privy Council to excise elements that might be construed as offensive to James VI, the portrait of Scotland that remained in the censored Holinshed's *Chronicles* was not a flattering one. It is typified by characterizations of the Scots as drunken barbarians, of Scottish government as ineffective and poorly organized, of a land racked by cycles of violent upheaval. At the same time, the "Historie of Scotland" offers some interesting perspectives on many of the issues that concerned Elizabethan England, such as the succession, the relationship between monarch and subject, and religious reform. The fact that these issues were presented within a Scottish rather than an English context probably allowed the authors of the "Historie of Scotland" a greater freedom to explore the various points of view surrounding them. Thynne's inclusion of a Catholic perspective on the Reformation and Holinshed's inclusion of the argument that a king could and should be deposed and executed for failing to rule properly could be construed as unpopular at best and dangerous at worst. Both authors avoid responsibility for these controversial ideas by clearly and often attributing them to their sources. Yet the final question remains, given the variety of sources from which they could have chosen, why did they choose these particular ones?

Chapter Six
Holinshed's *Chronicles* through the Centuries

The reputation of Holinshed's *Chronicles* has undergone a marked metamorphosis over the last four hundred years. An extremely popular work when it was first published, by the seventeenth century it was already considered outdated and inaccurate. In his "Satire 4," John Donne referred to its contents as "household trash." From the late eighteenth century through the twentieth century, the words of Stephen Booth sum up the general attitude toward Holinshed: "We care about Holinshed's *Chronicles* because Shakespeare read them."[1] Scholars of Tudor historiography have traditionally dismissed the *Chronicles* as a "badly articulated potpourri of diverse historical materials" (Levy, 182). Toward the end of the twentieth century, the importance of the *Chronicles* as a cultural resource was finally acknowledged, and scholars investigated the work as an important historical text in its own right. One critic proclaimed Holinshed "the greatest of the Elizabethan chronicles."[2]

When it first appeared in 1577, Holinshed's *Chronicles of England, Scotland, and Ireland* was the most comprehensive and lavish history ever published in England. Appearing in two volumes totaling almost three thousand pages, it was extensively illustrated with a series of woodcuts, some of them quite detailed. The first complete printed history of England composed as a continuous narrative and in the English language, it was regarded as the most authoritative history of its time.[3] The popularity of the text is verified by the fact that the sale of the first edition was large enough to persuade the printers to bring out an updated and even more extensive edition in 1587. While the 1587 edition was larger and more comprehensive than the 1577 edition, it was also less organized and balanced, and it lacked the 1577 illustrations. Despite its shortcomings, it also proved to be a well-respected success.

The *Chronicles'* notable influence on its own century is apparent in its role as a source for many of the literary authors of its day. Of course, the most notable was William Shakespeare, who borrowed historical material from the *Chronicles* for 13 of his 37 plays. Shakespeare used the later

"Historie of England" for *King John,* the Lancastrian plays *Richard II,*
1 Henry IV, 2 Henry IV, Henry V, 1 Henry VI, 2 Henry VI, 3 Henry VI, and
Richard III as well as *Henry VIII.* The "Historie of Scotland" provided
him with the material for *Macbeth,* and the semimythical ancient sections of the "Historie of England" inspired his retelling of *King Lear* and
Cymbeline.

Shakespeare was not the only Renaissance writer to draw on Holinshed as a literary source. The *Chronicles* supplied material for other history plays of the period, such as Marlowe's *Edward II* (ca. 1590) and for
such domestic tragedies as the anonymous *Arden of Feversham* (1591) and
A Warning for Fair Women (1599). Spenser used it as one of his sources for
"Briton moniments" found in Book II of the *Faerie Queene* (Canto X;
1590), and John Lyly incorporated passages from the "Description of
England" into *Euphues and his England* (1580). Even in the seventeenth,
eighteenth, and nineteenth centuries, long after it had ceased to be
regarded as a reliable historical text, authors continued to use Holinshed's *Chronicles* as a source of literary inspiration. Milton drew heavily
from the *Chronicles,* and its influence can be seen in *The Tenure of Kings*
and Magistrates (1649), *Eikonoklastes* (1649), and *History of Britain*
(1670).[4] George Lillo in his eighteenth-century dramatic reworking of
the infamous tale of Arden of Feversham turned to the *Chronicles* as had
his anonymous predecessor. Benjamin Disraeli used Holinshed's account
of the Wat Tyler rebellion as a source for an episode dealing with an
anarchic riot in his novel *Sybil; or, The Two Nations* (1845).[5]

Holinshed's *Chronicles* was the first, and yet ironically the last, complete and comprehensive history of England to be published. As F. J.
Levy has noted, "[T]he continual advances in the techniques of historical
research increased the amount of available information past all hope of
intelligibility" (Levy, 186). By the end of the first decade of the seventeenth century, Holinshed's *Chronicles* was considered dated and inaccurate and had been superseded by other general histories. In 1602, John
Clapham published his *Historie of England,* a narrative of Britain's early
history. In 1611, John Speed published his *History of Great Britain,* which
extended the narrative until the Tudor period. Both texts were unclut-
tered by the extraneous material and fabulous tales that characterized the
Chronicles' treatment of the same material. Clapham's and Speed's histories, although still technically chronicles in their format, reflect the historical methodology pioneered by Polydore Vergil early in the sixteenth
century, namely, the critical selection and evaluation of sources. By the
end of the century, this had become the standard methodology, as

demonstrated in the work of William Camden, the Society of Antiquaries, and the later writings of John Stow. Instead of including an extensive array of conflicting sources, thus allowing readers to evaluate the evidence and reach their own conclusions as did the compilers of Holinshed's *Chronicles,* Speed and Clapham chose what they considered the best authority and then wrote a straightforward narrative, based on that source. Their chronicle histories are characterized by compression and omission rather than by the expansion and inclusiveness of Holinshed's *Chronicles* (Levy, 197). Once considered the definitive history of the British Isles, Holinshed's *Chronicles* was completely discredited as a serious historical text less than fifty years after its publication.

The explosion of antiquarian study in the eighteenth century brought renewed interest to Holinshed's *Chronicles,* particularly in the recovery of the censored passages of the 1587 edition. A few copies of the unexpurgated 1587 edition existed, but these were held primarily in private collections. The desire of collectors of historical antiquities and curiosities to see or possess the scarce and costly canceled sheets led two groups of London booksellers to issue folio reprints in black-letter type that would enable collectors to "repair" the more commonly available castrated volumes. On 11 February 1723, Mears, Gyles, and Woodman advertised their reprint priced at five pounds, five shillings a set; five days later appeared Bateman and Cowse's advertisement of their 44-sheet reprint for fifty shillings. In 1728, another reprinting of the castrated sheets, also in folio size and black-letter type, edited by a Dr. Drake, appeared. All three issues included the same sheets: pages 421–24, 433–36, and 443–50 of the "Continuation of the Annales of Scotland" and pages 1328–31 and 1419–1574 of "The Continuation of the Historie of England." Many of the volumes of the 1587 edition that survive today are in eighteenth-century bindings. Those that contain the complete original text have probably been repaired in some way, either by making up the excised sheets from decrepit copies or by the use of one or another of the eighteenth-century reprints. The reconstruction and recombining of surviving copies of the *Chronicles* into new volumes that characterized early-eighteenth-century interest in Holinshed's *Chronicles* has made it exceedingly difficult for modern scholars to trace accurately the history of individual volumes (Castanien, 23–26).

In the late eighteenth century, a revival of interest in Shakespeare led to a newfound curiosity about the playwright's sources, but it was not until 1807 that the entire 1587 Holinshed finally appeared as a new edition. The project was undertaken as part of a large plan for reissuing sig-

nificant histories and chronicles from the sixteenth century. The editor
of the project was Sir Henry Ellis, Keeper of the Printed Books in the
British Museum and an experienced librarian with a particular interest
in antiquarian studies. The British Museum possessed several copies of
the second edition of Holinshed's *Chronicles,* apparently all excised.[6] It
appears that Ellis used an expurgated copy and then added those castrations that had been published between 1723 and 1728, since the advertisement for the edition states that all the castrations had been restored,
though it did not state the source of the text or the process of restoration
(Castanian, 25). Richard Lan, a London printer in Shoe Lane, published
the edition in 1807–1808.

The Ellis edition includes the title pages and dedications of the 1587
text as well as the original spelling and punctuation; however, Ellis took
a number of liberties with other aspects of the text. The excised pages
were restored to their respective places in the text, which at first may
seem like a positive improvement but on closer consideration reveals a
number of problems. First, this may have been the original text, but it
was not the text that was available to the *Chronicles'* original audience,
including Shakespeare and other borrowers from its extensive resources.
Second, Ellis's changes to the original text render it useless for certain
types of scholarly research. Because the 1807–1808 edition does not
indicate where expurgations originally occurred, and because its pagination has no relation to the 1587 text, any discussion of the expurgations
based on page numbers is purposeless. As Cyndia Clegg has noted in her
article "Which Holinshed? Holinshed's *Chronicles* at the Huntington
Library," "Unless we want to assume that alterations to the text are
irrelevant, working with Holinshed means working with the early editions."[7] Unfortunately, these early editions exist only in rare-book collections and therefore are not easily accessible.

Ellis and his publishers significantly changed the format of the *Chronicles'* text, choosing single columns and quarto-sized pages over the original double columns on folio-sized pages. Although this increased the
legibility of the text, it also increased the number of volumes to six,
necessitating different pagination and new indexes and increasing the
costliness of the edition (Snow 1976, 26). Lothrop Withington, a late-
nineteenth-century editor of William Harrison's *Description of England,*
complained that this edition was "an expensive reprint, far more inac-
cessible to the general reader than are the folios of the time of Elizabeth"
(Castanien, 25). It is a problem with this edition's reprint that remains
true to this day.

For some unknown reason, Ellis also rearranged the text by placing the "Description" and entire "Historie of Britain" before the Celtic subjects and inserting Scotland before Ireland, as it had appeared in the 1577 edition. In both the 1577 and the 1587 editions, the "Description of England" and the early "Historie of Britain" had appeared first. In the 1577 edition, the "Description" and "Historie of Scotland" and the "Description" and "Historie of Ireland" had followed, and finally the rest of the "Historie of England" after 1066. The 1587 edition differed from the earlier one in that it put the Irish section before the Scottish, but it followed its predecessor in placing the rest of the "Historie of England" after these two Celtic sections. Though Ellis's decision to reunite the two sections of the English history makes better editorial sense, it is yet another aspect of this edition that renders it even further removed from the text that circulated in the sixteenth century.

To this day and despite its many inaccuracies, Ellis's edition remains the only complete "modern" edition of Holinshed. In 1965 AMS Press issued a reprint of Ellis's edition, and in 1976 it issued a second printing of the same edition but with a new and highly informative introduction written by Vernon Snow. Although expensive, it is the 1807–1808 edition that is generally available in university libraries, primarily through its two reprints by AMS Press, and because this is the most widely available edition to both writer and audience, most scholars use it in their research. Annabel Patterson, after listing the edition's many problems, concisely sums up the dilemma in *Reading Holinshed's* Chronicles: "Yet in order to retain a system of citation that best serves the needs of today's readers, I shall continue to refer to the Ellis edition as a good *enough* source of the text of the 1587 edition" (Patterson 1994, 58).

Since the 1807–1808 edition, interest in reprinting the *Chronicles* has been limited primarily to those sections that deal with the social history of England during Elizabeth's reign or to those sections that served as a source for Shakespeare's plays. There are two editions that focus on the Celtic portions of the *Chronicles*. The earliest reprint of this sort appeared in 1805 and included the Scottish section of the 1587 Chronicles. It was entitled *The Scottish Chronicle: or a Complete History and Description of Scotland by the Reverend and Learned Mr. Raphael Hollingshead* (Abroath, 1805). The edition was carelessly prepared, confusing the life and work of Raphael Holinshed with those of William Harrison and failing to note the publication history of the Scottish history or the fact that it included the expurgated text.

In 1979, a limited edition of the 1577 "Description" and "Historie of Ireland," entitled *Holinshed's Irish Chronicle,* was published by Dolmen editions.[8] Edited by Liam Miller and Eileen Power, the text includes both the original and expurgated passages from Stanyhurst's history and the original woodcut illustrations. Although the text has been reformatted and the pagination changed, this edition is a valuable scholarly resource for a variety of reasons. Because it is the only reprint ever published of any section of the 1577 *Chronicles,* it enables the reader to compare at least the Irish text of both the 1577 and the 1587 editions without having to resort to locating the original sixteenth-century editions. Its inclusion of the original woodcuts, deleted from the 1587 edition, also makes available to a wider audience this important element of the 1577 edition.

Another section of the *Chronicles,* Harrison's "Description of England," has appeared in a number of editions in the last two centuries, none of which presents either the 1577 or the 1587 version in its original or entire form. The first, edited by Frederick J. Furnivall, was published in a two-volume set in 1877 and was entitled, tellingly enough, *Harrison's Description of England in Shakespeare's Youth.* This is not a complete edition; it contains only a few fragments from the first book along with the second and third books of the "Description." Furnivall did not consider the first book of enough interest to include in his edition. It was published for the New Shakespeare Society, which Furnivall had founded and directed. As with most later editors of Holinshed's *Chronicles,* Furnivall based his interest in the "Description" primarily on his interest in Shakespeare. He notes in his foreword, "The [Description] is full of interest not only to every Shakespeare student, but to every reader of English history." Furnivall combined the 1577 and 1587 versions of the "Description," using brackets to indicate material added in revision but including no commentary or analysis of the changes. He also supplemented Harrison's marginal annotations with his own, a device that tends to confuse modern readers. Another late-nineteenth-century edition of Harrison's "Description," which again includes only sections of the text, was edited by Lothrop E. Withington. In 1968, George Edelen reedited the "Description" for the Folger Shakespeare Library. Edelen basically included the same material that Furnivall had, except that he modernized the spelling and did not collate the two sixteenth-century editions of Holinshed as Furnivall had done. He added some more sections from the first book and deleted some of the material that Furnivall had earlier included. In this sense, Edelen's text is not much of an improvement over its nineteenth-century counterparts.

The fragmentation and reorganization of the original Holinshed appears also in editions focused on the "Historie of England" as used by Shakespeare in his plays. It has long been the general assumption that one reads Holinshed only as a source for Shakespeare. The numerous editions of Shakespeare's Holinshed that include only brief excerpts from the 1587 "Historie of England" are the only editions of Holinshed to be found on many university and college library shelves. The format of these texts varies from Boswell-Stone's *Shakespeare's Holinshed: The Chronicle and the Historical Plays Compared* (1896), in which abbreviated historical excerpts are arranged in the chronological order of Shakespeare's plays and the action of the plays that they illustrate is briefly described, to Richard Hosley's *Shakespeare's Holinshed* (1968), which arranges the excerpts in the order found in the *Chronicles* but still in a much abbreviated form. Although these texts well serve to illustrate how Shakespeare adapted his source material to his own creative work, they are useless for any serious study of the *Chronicles* itself.

The most recent edition of Holinshed is a 1998 facsimile edition of that portion of the 1587 English history dealing with Elizabeth's reign, edited by Cyndia Clegg. Although again it deals with only a portion of the vast "Historie of England," it is one of the few modern editions of the English section of the *Chronicles* that presents the entire narrative rather than fragmented excerpts or conflations of the two editions, thus serving as a valuable scholarly tool for students of the Elizabethan era. Its facsimile format also makes more widely available to modern readers an example of how the sixteenth-century *Chronicles* first appeared.

Michael Tomlinson points out that "[t]he relationship between Shakespeare's history plays and the chronicles of Halle and Holinshed is one of the oldest concerns of Shakespearean criticism."[9] One of the earlier and most significant examples of this critical tendency appears in the work of Boswell-Stone. Late in the nineteenth century Boswell-Stone, after comparing the texts of several of Shakespeare's plays with both the 1577 and the 1587 editions of Holinshed's *Chronicles,* concluded that Shakespeare must have used the 1587 edition. He based his conclusions on the fact that certain key words and phrases employed in *Richard II, Henry IV, Henry V, Henry VI,* and *Richard III* not evident in the 1577 edition appeared in the 1587 edition. From this comparative data Boswell-Stone deduced that several other plays, including *Lear, Cymbeline, King John,* and *Henry VIII,* were also based on the second edition. Boswell-Stone's conclusions account for the fact that almost all critical work done on the *Chronicles* focuses on the 1587 rather than the 1577 edition;

however, as Arthur Kinney has convincingly demonstrated, such assumptions cannot always be taken at face value. The Kinney proves that Shakespeare must have consulted the 1577 rather than the 1587 edition of Holinshed's chronicles by pointing out that some of the most vivid images in the play can be found in no other source but the woodcuts of the 1577 edition (Kinney, 32–37).

Most historians who specialize in the early modern era have traditionally dismissed the *Chronicles* as a historical work because of its lack of selectivity and analysis. The emphasis on the *Chronicles'* role as a Shakespearean source rather than a historical document in its own right unfortunately appears in the work of not only literary but historical scholars as well. Early in the twentieth century, C. L. Kingsford claimed that the only value of Holinshed's *Chronicles* lay in its role as a Shakespearean source: "It is perhaps more due to the service which he rendered to Shakespeare than to any merit of his own that Holinshed has long overshadowed Hall and Stow as an historian of the fifteenth century . . . though his *Chronicles* were a meritorious compilation, which in default of printed originals were long of much historical value, their greatest interest now consists in their literary associations" (Kingsford 1913, 274).

F. J. Levy, whose *Tudor Historical Thought* is still considered the definitive work on the subject, also dismisses the *Chronicles* as a historical work because of its lack of selectivity and analysis, and like Kingsford he finds its only saving grace its role as some great literary warehouse from which better authors could choose and fashion what they needed:

> ". . . . Holinshed's *Historie* demonstrated most fully the idea that history could be written by agglomeration. Holinshed's wide reading in the source of English history was used not to determine the truth in matters doubtful but merely to add more and more detail . . . The result of this accumulation was that there was virtually no attempt to find the cause of events: without saying so, Holinshed leaves us with the impression that establishing causality is also the task of the reader. In a way, this made him the ideal source for the playwrights; everything needful (and a great deal more) was included, but the "construction," the ordering of events, was left to others, who thus could make of the multitudinous facts what they would. (Levy, 84)

In the work of both literary and historical scholars, the critical attention devoted to Holinshed has traditionally focused on the text's relationship to Shakespeare and its role as a literary source.

Only within the last 40 years of the twentieth century has the *Chronicles* received much critical attention in its own right. Some exciting work has been done on the ways that it reflects issues of censorship and popular culture in sixteenth-century England. Two articles that appeared during the 1950s make a significant step forward in scholarship of the *Chronicles*. Sarah Dodson's "Abraham Fleming, Writer and Editor" and William Miller's "Abraham Fleming: Editor of Shakespeare's Holinshed" established that it was Abraham Fleming, and not John Hooker alias Vowell as previously believed, who was the editor of the 1587 edition. This view was later verified in two articles by Elizabeth Story Donno, "Abraham Fleming: A Learned Corrector in 1586–87," and "Some Aspects of Shakespeare's Holinshed," through a close examination of proof texts located in the Huntington Library in San Marino. It is now generally accepted that Fleming was indeed the editor of the 1587 *Chronicles*.

Although most current scholars of Tudor historical thought continue to dismiss the *Chronicles* as undisciplined, disorganized, and unanalytical, recent work, particularly by Cyndia Clegg, Elizabeth Story Donno, and Annabel Patterson, have called for a reconsideration of the *Chronicles* as a valuable resource for the exploration of censorship and the concept of knowledge in early modern England. Stephen Booth first mentions the topic of censorship in his *Book Called Holinshed's Chronicles,* but it received its fullest treatment in Anne Castanien's Ph.D. dissertation, "Censorship and Historiography in Elizabethan England: The Expurgation of Holinshed's *Chronicles,*" which, although it remains unpublished, is still the most widely cited text on this topic. Clegg and Donno have also touched on the censorship issue in their respective articles, "Which Holinshed? Holinshed's *Chronicles* at the Huntington Library" and "Some Aspects of Shakespeare's Holinshed," while both Clegg and Annabel Patterson devote a chapter to it in their respective studies *Press Censorship in Elizabethan England* and *Reading Holinshed's* Chronicles (Clegg 1997, 138–69; Patterson 1994, 234–63). In Patterson's groundbreaking work, the first full-length study of the *Chronicles,* she convincingly argues that the *Chronicles* must be read in its own right as an important cultural history, not only for what it reveals to us about early modern censorship but also for the insights that it conveys into the way that the Elizabethan middle class understood their society.

Recent criticism has also revealed that the multivocality of the *Chronicles* even today results in a variety of readings, often contradictory. Whereas some critics, such as Mark Benbow, Michael Tomlinson, and

Jurgen Beers, have argued that Holinshed's *Chronicles* represents the Tudor party line in its orthodox treatment of rebellion and authority and its glorification of the Tudor myth, other critics, such as Annabel Patterson, have pointed to the subtly subversive nature of the text, which questions rather than blindly supports the ideology of those in power.

Much work remains to be done on the *Chronicles*. Modern and accurate editions of both the 1577 and the 1587 *Chronicles* are needed to facilitate careful and thorough scholarship. The Scottish and Irish sections of the work have been all but ignored, even though their cultural significance, given that they were produced in the time of a possible Scottish succession and the colonization of Ireland, cannot be overestimated. The only study of the Irish portion, a particularly rich source of information on sixteenth-century English colonialism, which includes one of the few sixteenth-century English-language works on Ireland written by a native-born Irishman, albeit an Anglo-Irish one, is the introduction to the 1979 edition of the 1577 Holinshed mentioned earlier. Except for examinations of its influence on *Macbeth,* no significant study has been undertaken of the "Chronicles of Scotland." I am hopeful that the pioneering work of Castanien, Clegg, Donno, and Patterson will lead to a greater interest in the *Chronicles* as a valuable source of cultural information about sixteenth-century England, Ireland, and Scotland.

Notes and References

Preface

    1. These collections include W. G. Boswell-Stone, *Shakespeare's Holinshed: The Chronicle and the Historical Plays Compared* (1896; reprint, New York: Benjamin Blom, 1966); Richard Hosley, *Shakespeare's Holinshed: An Edition of Holinshed's "Chronicles," 1587* (New York: Putnam, 1968); Allardyce Nicoll and Josephine Nicoll, *Holinshed's "Chronicle" as Used in Shakespeare's Plays* (London: J. M. Dent and Sons, 1927); and R. S. Wallace and Alma Hansen, *Holinshed's "Chronicles"* (London: Clarendon Press, 1923).

    2. F. J. Levy, *Tudor Historical Thought* (San Marino, Calif.: Huntington Library Press, 1967), 183–84; hereafter cited in text.

    3. Annabel Patterson, *Reading Holinshed's "Chronicles"* (Chicago: University of Chicago Press, 1994); hereafter cited in text as Patterson 1994.

    4. Cyndia Susan Clegg, "The Review and Reform of Holinshed's *Chronicles*: 'Reporte of matters of later yeers that concern the State' " in *Press Censorship in Elizabethan England* (Cambridge: Cambridge University Press, 1997); hereafter cited in text as Clegg 1997.

    5. Raphael Holinshed, *Holinshed's Irish Chronicle,* ed. Liam Miller and Eileen Power, Dolmen Editions (Atlantic Highlands, N.J.: Humanities Press, 1979); hereafter cited in text as *Irish,* followed by the volume and page numbers. All other references to the 1577 edition of Holinshed's *Chronicles* will be hereafter cited in text as Holin. 1577, followed by the volume and folio numbers.

    6. Raphael Holinshed, *Holinshed's Chronicles of England, Scotland, and Ireland,* ed. Henry Ellis, 6 vols. (1807–1808; reprint with an introduction by Vernon Snow, New York: AMS Press, 1965, 1976); hereafter cited in text as *Chronicles,* followed by the volume and page numbers.

Chapter One

    1. See Levy, 79–123, and May McKisack, *Medieval History in the Tudor Age* (Oxford: Clarendon Press, 1971), 120–21.

    2. For a discussion of this, see Peter Burke, *The Renaissance Sense of the Past* (London: Edward Arnold, 1969), 1–2; and Phyllis Rackin's *Stages of History: Shakespeare's English Chronicles* (Ithaca, N.Y.: Cornell University Press, 1990), 5–12.

    3. See Sarah Dodson, "Abraham Fleming, Writer and Editor," *University of Texas Studies in English* 34 (1955): 51–60; William E. Miller, "Abraham

Fleming: Editor of Shakespeare's Holinshed," *Texas Studies in Literature and Language* 1 (1959–1960): 89–100; and Elizabeth Story Donno's two articles, "Abraham Fleming: A Learned Corrector in 1586–87," *Studies in Bibliography* 42 (1989): 200–11, hereafter cited in text as Donno 1989; and "Some Aspects of Shakespeare's Holinshed," *Huntington Library Quarterly* 50, no. 3 (Summer 1987): 229–48; hereafter cited in text as Donno 1987.

    4.   Holinshed's given name also appears as Ralph and his surname as Hollingshead or Holinshead in documentary sources. *Dictionary of National Biography* (London: Oxford University Press, H. Milford 1937–1938) (hereafter cited as *DNB*) 9: 1024–26.

    5.   See G. J. R. Parry, *A Protestant Vision: William Harrison and the Reformation of Elizabethan England* (Cambridge: Cambridge University Press, 1987a), 7; hereafter cited in text.

    6.   Blayney, Peter W. M., *The Bookshops in Paul's Cross Churchyard,* Occasional Papers of the Bibliographical Society, no. 5 (London: Bibliographical Society, 1990), 19.

    7.   See "Reyner Wolfe," *DNB* 21 (1937–1938): 775 and Charles Lethbridge Kingsford's introduction to *A Survey of London by John Stow* (Oxford: Clarendon Press, 1908), xxi; hereafter cited in text as Kingsford 1908.

    8.   See Georges Edelen, "William Harrison (1535–1593)," *Studies in the Renaissance* 9 (1962): 258–61.

    9.   See "William Harrison," *DNB* 9: 46–47, and George Edelen's introduction to William Harrison's *Description of England,* ed. Georges Edelen (New York: Cornell University Press, 1968), xxviii; Edelen is hereafter cited in text.

    10.   Campion's work was not published until 1633, almost 75 years after it was written, under the title *Two Bokes of the Historie of Ireland.*

    11.   See Colm Lennon, *Richard Stanihurst the Dubliner 1547–1618* (Blackrock, County Dublin: Irish Academic Press, 1981), 36, 40–41.

    12.   See "Richard Stanyhurst," *DNB* 18 (1937–1938): 976–77.

    13.   See G. J. R. Parry, "John Stow's Unpublished 'Historie of this Island': Amity and Enmity amongst Sixteenth-Century Scholars," *English Historical Review* 102, no. 404 (July 1987b), 641–42.

    14.   See Barrett Beer, "John Stow and Tudor Rebellions, 1549–1569," *Journal of British Studies* 27 (1988): 353.

    15.   See "John Stow," *DNB* 19 (1937–1938): 3–4.

    16.   See Vernon Snow, *Parliament in Elizabethan England: John Hooker's 'Order and Usage'* (New Haven, CT: Yale University Press, 1977), 3–19; hereafter cited in text.

    17.   See "John Hooker," *DNB* 9 (1937–1938): 1181–93.

    18.   See "Abraham Fleming," *DNB* 7 (1937–1938): 273.

    19.   See "Francis Thynne," *DNB* 19 (1937–1938): 844–45.

    20.   E. Gordon Duff, *A Century of the English Book Trade* (London: Printed for the Bibliographical Society by Blades, East and Blades, 1905), 35, 67–68.

21.   Cyndia Susan Clegg, "Which Holinshed? Holinshed's *Chronicles* at the Huntington Library," *Huntington Library Quarterly* 55, no. 4 (Fall 1992): 562.

22.   See R. B. McKerrow, *A Dictionary of Printers and Booksellers in England, Scotland and Ireland, and of Foreign Printers of English Books 1557–1640* (London: The Bibliographical Society, 1968), 35; hereafter cited in text.

23.   See "Henry Denham," *DNB* 5 (1937–1938): 793.

24.   See "Ralph Newbery," *DNB* 14 (1937–1938): 314.

25.   See Annabel Patterson, "Rethinking Tudor Historiography," *South Atlantic Quarterly* 92, no. 2 (Spring 1993): 190, 207.

Chapter Two

1.   For varying arguments concerning Holinshed's portrait of Richard II, see H. A. Kelly, *Divine Providence in the England of Shakespeare's Histories* (Cambridge: Harvard University Press, 1970), 139–42, and Patterson, 1994, 112–17.

2.   I disagree with F. J. Levy's assertion that Holinshed's sole purpose was to supply a moral lesson. In fact, the "Historie of England" contains important elements of what Levy terms the "politic history." See Levy, 184, 237–85.

3.   Both Annabel Patterson's *Reading Holinshed's* Chronicles and Liam Miller and Eileen Power's introduction to *Holinshed's Irish Chronicle* provide detailed discussions of the 1577 woodcuts. See Patterson, 1994, 56–57; and Miller and Power, xvii–xviii.

4.   John Guy, *Tudor England* (Oxford: Oxford University Press, 1988), 247; hereafter cited in text.

5.   See R. Mark Benbow, "The Providential Theory of Historical Causation in Holinshed's *Chronicles*: 1577 and 1587," *Texas Studies in Literature and Language* 1 (1959): 264–76; as well as Dodson; and Donno, 1989.

6.   Richard Helgerson, *Forms of Nationhood: The Elizabethan Writing of England* (Chicago: University of Chicago Press, 1992), 252; hereafter cited in text.

7.   Although I do not agree with all of Benbow's analysis, I do believe that he is correct in pointing out the teleological nature of the 1587 "Historie of England."

8.   See Anne Castanien, "Censorship and Historiography in Elizabethan England: The Expurgation of Holinshed's *Chronicles,*" (Ph.D. diss., University of California, Davis, 1970), 277–78. See also Clegg, 1997, 143–45.

9.   *Acts of the Privy Council, 1586–1587,* ed. J. R. Dasent (London, 1890–1907), vol. xiv, 311–12; hereafter cited in text as *APC,* followed by volume and page numbers.

Chapter Three

1.   Not until Christopher Saxton's county maps were published in 1579 did a collection of detailed and accurate maps exist in England. These

maps were first printed as individual sheets between 1574 and 1578, thus accounting for both Holinshed's and Harrison's references to them as such in the 1577 *Chronicles.* For a discussion of Saxon's maps, see Helgerson, 107–14.

2. Leland's research, or "Itinerary," as it has come to be known, was not published until 1710–1712 by Thomas Hearne, librarian of the Bodleian library. See Thomas Kendrick, foreword to vol. 1 of *The Itinerary of John Leland,* ed. Lucy Tollman Smith (Carbondale, Ill.: Southern Illinois University Press, 1964), xix.

3. Thomas Seckford was Saxton's patron. See Helgerson, 108–111.

4. G. J. R. Parry, "William Harrison and Holinshed's *Chronicles,*" *Historical Journal* 27, no. 4 (1984): 799.

5. See Keith Wrightson, *English Society 1580–1680* (New Brunswick, N.J.: Rutgers University Press, 1982), 121–48. Hereafter cited in text.

Chapter Four

1. See note 10 to chapter 1.

2. See James P. Meyers, *Elizabethan Ireland: A Selection of Writings by Elizabethan Writers on Ireland* (Hamden, Conn.: Archon Books, 1983), 4.

3. For discussions on the possible motives for the cancellations see Castanien, 91; Clegg 1997, 139–140; *Irish,* xvi–xvii; and Patterson 1994, 11–12.

4. Mary O'Down, "Gaelic Economy and Society," in *Natives and Newcomers: Essays on the Making of Irish Colonial Society,* ed. Ciaran Brady and Raymond Gillespie (Dublin: Irish Academic Press, 1986), 139.

5. R. Dudley Edwards, *Ireland in the Age of the Tudors* (London: Croom Helm, 1977), 116.

6. For a detailed study of Hooker's "Order and Usage" see Snow 1977.

7. Richard Beacon, introduction to *Solon his follie* (1594), ed. Clare Carroll and Vincent Carey (Binghamton, N.Y.: Center for Medieval and Early Renaissance Studies, 1996), xxvi–xxvii.

Chapter Five

1. Hector Boece, *The Chronicle of Scotland,* trans. John Bellenden (1531), ed. R. W. Chambers and Edith C. Batho (Edinburgh: Scottish Text Society, 3rd series, vol. 1, no 10, 1936).

2. For a discussion of these specifically Scottish woodcuts and their influence on Shakespeare's *Macbeth,* see Arthur F. Kinney's "Scottish History, the Union of the Crowns and the Issue of Right Rule: The Case of Shakespeare's *Macbeth*" in *Renaissance Culture in Context: Theory and Practice,* ed. Jean R. Brink and William F. Gentrup (Aldershot, England: Scolar Press, 1993), 18–53. Hereafter cited in text.

3. J. B. Black, "Boece's 'Scotorum Historiae,' " in *University of Aberdeen Quartercentenary of the Death of Hector Boece, First Principal of the University* (Aberdeen: The University Press, 1936), 43. Hereafter cited in text.

4. See I. D. McFarlane, *Buchanan* (London: Duckworth, 1981), 419; and Black, 43.

5. John Knox, *History of the Reformation in Scotland,* ed. William Croft Dickinson, 2 vols. (New York: Philosophical Library, 1950).

Chapter Six

1. Stephen Booth, *The Book Called Holinshed's Chronicles: An Account of Its Inception, Purpose, Contributors, Contents, Publication, Revision, and Influence on William Shakespeare* (San Francisco: The Book Club, 1968), 72.

2. Annabel Patterson, "Local Knowledge: 'Popular' Representation in Elizabethan Historiography," in *Place and Displacement in the Renaissance,* ed. Alvin Vos (Binghamton, N.Y.: Medieval and Renaissance Texts and Studies, 1995), 87.

3. Charles Lethbridge Kingsford, *English Historical Literature in the Fifteenth Century* (Oxford: Clarendon Press, 1913), 271. Hereafter cited in text as Kingsford 1913.

4. I thank Steve Buhler of the University of Nebraska, Lincoln, for pointing out these examples of Milton's use of Holinshed's *Chronicles.*

5. See Lois E. Bueler, "Disraeli's *Sybil* and Holinshed's *Chronicles,*" *Victorian Newsletter* 54 (Fall 1978): 17–19.

6. See Vernon F. Snow, "Four Centuries of Holinshed's Chronicles," *Courier* 13, no. 3–4 (1976): 24. Hereafter cited in text as Snow 1976.

7. Cyndia Susan Clegg, "Which Holinshed? Holinshed's *Chronicles* at the Huntington Library," *Huntington Library Quarterly* 55, no. 4 (Fall 1992): 567.

8. See note 5 to the preface.

9. Michael Tomlinson, "Shakespeare and the Chronicles Reassessed," *Literature and History* 10, no. 1 (1984): 46.

Selected Bibliography

Primary Works

Holinshed, Raphael. *The Chronicles of England, Scotlande, and Irelande.* 3 vols. London, 1577.

———. *The Chronicles of England, Ireland, and Scotland.* 3 vols. London, 1587.

Modern editions

Boswell-Stone, W. G. *Shakespeare's Holinshed: The Chronicle and the Historical Plays Compared.* 1896. Reprint, New York: Benjamin Blom, 1966. Historical excerpts from the 1587 *Chronicles* are arranged in the order of Shakespeare's dramas and accompanied by brief descriptions of the plays' action.

Furnivall, Frederick. *Harrison's Description of England in Shakspere's Youth.* 2 vols. London: 1877. Includes a few brief excerpts from the first book and the entire second and third books of Harrison's "Description." Conflates the 1577 and 1587 editions of the "Description."

Harrison, William. *The Description of England.* Edited by Georges Edelen. The Folger Shakespeare Library. New York: Cornell University Press, 1968. Includes excerpts from the first book, and, with the exception of what the editor judged to be "four lengthy and readily detachable digressions," the entire second and third books of the 1587 "Description." Includes an introduction and notes.

Holinshed, Raphael. *Holinshed's Chronicles of England, Scotland, and Ireland.* Edited by Henry Ellis. 6 vols. London: 1807–1808; reprint with an introduction by Vernon Snow, New York: AMS Press, 1965, 1976. The only modern edition of the entire 1587 *Chronicles.* Includes the canceled passages of the original text.

———. *Holinshed's Irish Chronicle.* Edited by Liam Miller and Eileen Power. Dolmen Editions. Atlantic Highlands, N.J.: Humanities Press, 1979. A modern edition of the 1577 *Irish Chronicle,* complete with introduction, woodcuts, original text, and the text of the substituted leaves.

———. *The Scottish Chronicle; or a complete history and description of Scotland by the Reverend and Learned Mr. Raphael Holingshed.* Arbroath, Scotland: 1805. The Scottish portion of the 1587 edition. Contains numerous errors, such as confusing Holinshed's life and work with Harrison's.

———. *The peaceable and prosperous regiment of blessed Queene Elisabeth: A Facsimile from Holinshed's Chronicles (1587).* Edited by Cyndia Susan Clegg. San

Marino, Calif.: Huntington Library Press, 1998. A facsimile edition of the 1587 narrative of Elizabeth's reign accompanied by an introduction and notes.

Hosley, Richard, ed. *Shakespeare's Holinshed: An Edition of Holinshed's Chronicles, 1587.* New York: Putnam, 1968. Selections from the 1587 *Chronicles* used by Shakespeare in his plays.

Nicoll, Allardyce and Josephine. *Holinshed's Chronicle as Used in Shakespeare's Plays.* London: J. M. Dent and Sons, 1927. Fragments from the 1587 *Chronicles* used by Shakespeare in his plays. Contains erroneous information.

Wallace, R. S., and Alma Hansen, ed. *Holinshed's Chronicles.* London: Clarendon Press, 1923. Excerpts from the *Chronicles* used by Shakespeare in his history plays.

Withington, Lothrop, ed. *Elizabethan England: From "A Description of England" by William Harrison (In Holinshed's Chronicles)* London, n.d. Selections from William Harrison's "Description of England."

Secondary Sources

Beer, Jurgen. "The Image of a King: Henry VIII in the Tudor Chronicles of Edward Hall and Raphael Holinshed." In *History, Historiography and Literature,* edited by Uwe Baumann, 129–50. Frankfurt: Peter Lang, 1992. Argues that the chronicles of Hall and Holinshed embody the "official view" of history in their depiction of Henry VIII's reign and their celebration of the "Tudor myth." Contrasts the *Chronicles'* concentration on courtly splendor and chivalric deeds early in Henry's reign with their more factual account of Henry's forceful implementation of power in his later years.

Benbow, R. Mark. "The Providential Theory of Historical Causation in Holinshed's *Chronicles*: 1577 and 1587." *Texas Studies in Literature and Language* 1 (1959): 264–76. A study of the historical points of view in the 1577 and 1587 "Historie of England." Argues that the 1587 text presents history as a working out of God's providence.

Booth, Stephen. *The Book Called Holinshed's Chronicles: An Account of Its Inception, Purpose, Contributors, Contents, Publication, Revision, and Influence on William Shakespeare.* San Francisco: The Book Club, 1968. A background history of the *Chronicles* accompanied by a discussion of the bibliographical problems created by the censorship of the 1587 edition. Each copy of this limited edition text includes a leaf of the original 1587 *Chronicles.*

Boyd, Brian. "*King John* and *The Troublesome Raigne*: Sources, Structure, Sequence." *Philological Quarterly* 74, no. 1 (Winter 1995): 37–56. Argues that Shakespeare's *King John* is the source of the anonymous *The Troublesome Raigne of King John* and not vice versa. Demonstrates how the character of Philip Falconbridge is a composite of four different bastards found in Holinshed's "Historie of England."

Bueler, Lois E. "Disraeli's *Sybil* and Holinshed's *Chronicles*." *Victorian Newsletter* 54 (Fall 1978): 17–19. Suggests that the handling of popular insurrection in *Sybil* is indebted to Tudor chronicle sources. Particularly noteworthy is that the death of Simon Hatton is almost identical to an episode in Holinshed's account of the Wat Tyler rebellion.

Castanien, Anne. "Censorship and Historiography in Elizabethan England: The Expurgation of Holinshed's *Chronicles*." Ph.D. diss., University of California, Davis, 1970. A comprehensive and detailed examination of the effects of Elizabethan press censorship on the preparation and publication of the *Chronicles*.

Clegg, Cyndia Susan. "Which Holinshed? Holinshed's *Chronicles* at the Huntington Library." *Huntington Library Quarterly* 55, no. 4 (Fall 1992): 559–77. A description of the various 1577 and 1587 editions available at the Huntington Library, San Marino, California.

———. "The Review and Reform of Holinshed's *Chronicles*: 'Reporte of matters of later yeers that concern the State' " In *Press Censorship in Elizabethan England*. Cambridge: Cambridge University Press, 1997. Argues that the *Chronicles* enjoyed a different status from other texts censored by Elizabeth's government and that their censorship represented the government's attempts to construct a favorable domestic and international image.

Dodson, Sarah. "Abraham Fleming, Writer and Editor." *University of Texas Studies in English* 34 (1955): 51–60. A biographical account of Fleming's life and scholarship. Argues that Fleming supervised the construction of the 1587 "Historie of England."

Donno, Elizabeth Story. "Abraham Fleming: A Learned Corrector in 1586–87." *Studies in Bibliography* 42 (1989): 200–11. Based on the evidence provided by two bound copies of the *Chronicles'* proof sheets at the Huntington Library, demonstrates the extensive contributions of Abraham Fleming to the 1587 edition. Concentrates on Fleming's role as "corrector" for the text. Includes a biography of Fleming and a brief description of his various other works.

———. "Some Aspects of Shakespeare's Holinshed." *Huntington Library Quarterly* 50, no.3 (Summer 1987): 229–48. Discusses Fleming's life and his contribution to the 1587 *Chronicles* as demonstrated by the Huntington Library's proof copies.

Hardin, Richard F. "Chronicles and Mythmaking in Shakespeare's Joan of Arc." *Shakespeare Survey* 42 (1990): 25–35. Notes the more detailed and negative portrayal of Joan of Arc in the 1587 Holinshed as opposed to that of the 1577 edition. Argues that Shakespeare's particularly unflattering portrait of Joan in *1 Henry VI* is based only in part on the chronicles and that he "enthusiastically compounded the felony" in defaming Joan far more than his sources.

Helgerson, Richard. *Forms of Nationhood: The Elizabethan Writing of England.* Chicago: University of Chicago Press, 1992. A study of the various ways in which later Elizabethan authors constructed the concept of an English nation in their writings.

Kelen, Sarah A. " 'It Is Dangerous (Gentle Reader)': Censorship, Holinshed's *Chronicle*, and the Politics of Control." *Sixteenth Century Journal* 27, no. 3 (Fall 1996): 705–20. Argues that the control of texts, authors, and history is the dominant motif that organizes and unifies the 1587 *Chronicles*.

Kinney, Arthur F. "Scottish History, the Union of the Crowns and the Issue of Right Rule: The Case of Shakespeare's *Macbeth*." In *Renaissance Culture in Context: Theory and Practice,* edited by Jean R. Brink and William F. Gentrup, 18–53. Aldershot, England: Scolar Press, 1993. Points out a number of previously unnoticed parallels between the "Historie of Scotland," *Macbeth,* and James I's reign. Demonstrates how the play's digression on James's ancestry, included in Holinshed's account of Macbeth's reign, provided Shakespeare with a means of commenting on James's own political ambitions and on the dangers of imperialist and absolutist thought through its depiction of a tyrant who aspired to absolute power.

Levy, F. J. *Tudor Historical Thought.* San Marino, Calif.: Huntington Library Press, 1967. An authoritative study of Tudor historiography.

Matheson, Lister M. "English Chronicle Contexts for Shakespeare's Death of Richard II." In *From Page to Performance: Essays in Early English Drama,* edited by John A. Alford, 195–219. East Lansing: Michigan State University Press, 1995. Explains how Shakespeare chose from among the conflicting reports of Richard II's death portrayed in Hall's and Holinshed's chronicle histories to construct his own version of the regicide.

Miller, William E. "Abraham Fleming: Editor of Shakespeare's Holinshed." *Texas Studies in Literature and Language* 1 (1959–1960): 89–100. Supports and expands Dodson's argument that Abraham Fleming was the editor of the 1587 "Historie of England." Presents evidence that Fleming may have been the editor of the entire 1587 *Chronicles*.

Parry, G. J. R. "John Stow's Unpublished 'Historie of this Iland': Amity and Enmity Amongst Sixteenth-Century Scholars." *English Historical Review* 102, no. 404 (July 1987): 633–47. Discusses Stow's contributions to the *Chronicles* and his relationship with William Harrison.

———. "William Harrison and Holinshed's *Chronicles*." *Historical Journal* 27, no. 4 (1984) 789–810. Examines Harrison's role in the creation of the *Chronicles*. Argues that Harrison's "Description of England" was a deviation from the main focus of his own work.

Patterson, Annabel. "Local Knowledge: 'Popular' Representation in Elizabethan Historiography." In *Place and Displacement in the Renaissance,* edited by Alvin Vos, 87–106. Binghamton, N.Y.: Medieval and Renaissance Texts and Studies, 1995. Argues that the authors of the *Chronicles* shared a concern for justice and fairness that is revealed through anecdotes of popular protest and unjust law enforcement.

————. *Reading Holinshed's* Chronicles. Chicago: University of Chicago Press, 1994. The first major book-length study of the *Chronicles*. Demonstrates the importance of the *Chronicles* as a cultural history of the sixteenth century.

————. "Rethinking Tudor Historiography." *South Atlantic Quarterly* 92, no. 2 (Spring 1993): 185–208. Defense of the *Chronicles* as a significant sixteenth-century historiographical achievement.

Snow, Vernon F. "Four Centuries of Holinshed's Chronicles (1577–1977)." *Courier* 13, no. 3–4 (1976): 3–27. A history of the *Chronicles'* various editions, from the original 1577 text through the second AMS reprint of Henry Ellis's 1807–1808 edition in 1976.

Tomlinson, Michael. "Shakespeare and the Chronicles Reassessed." *Literature and History* 10, no. 1 (1984): 46–58. Argues that although Shakespeare's history plays are based on Hall's and Holinshed's chronicle histories, Shakespeare's attitude toward monarchy, authority, and rebellion diverge from what the author believes to be the chronicles' orthodox treatment of these political issues.

Woodson, William C. "Iago's Name in *Holinshed* and the Lost English Source of *Othello*." *Notes and Queries* 25 (1978): 146–47. Notes that in Holinshed's *Chronicles,* shortly after the reign of King Leir, appears the story of King Iago, who ruled 28 years and that the combination of the name and the 28 years (Shakespeare's Iago is described as having "look'd upon the world for four times seven years" [I.iii.311–12]) points to Holinshed, and not a lost English source, as having provided the name and age for Iago.

Yamada, Naomichi. "The Tragedy of the Man Who 'Bought A Glass' in *King Richard III*: Shakespeare's Reinterpretation of Holinshed—(I)." *Hitotsubashi Journal of Arts and Sciences* 34, no. 1 (1993): 1–23; 35, no. 1 (1994): 1–31. Discusses how Shakespeare departs from the 1587 Holinshed in his portrayal of Richard III. Argues that Shakespeare develops interpersonal dynamics between Richard and the other characters in the play through dialogue not found in Holinshed.

Index

160   INDEX

Holinshed's Chronicles of England, Ireland, and Scotland. See *Chronicles of England, Ireland, and Scotland*
Holinshed's Irish Chronicle Miller and Power), 140
Hollinshed of Cophurst, 3
Honorius, Pope, 31–32
Hooker, John, 3, 12–13, 76; and "Description of Scotland," 111; and Fleming, Abraham, 14, 15; and "Historie of England," 1587 edition, 41, 45; and "Historie of Ireland," 1587 edition, 96–107; "Order and Usage of Keeping the Parliaments in England," 13, 101
Hooker, Richard, 12
Hosley, Richard, 141
Huntington Library, 143

Inns of Court, 7
Ireland. See *Chronicles of England, Ireland, and Scotland*; "Description of Ireland"; "Historie of Ireland"
Irish House of Commons, 13, 101
Irish language, 79–80, 82
Irish Parliament, 12, 13, 101
Irishry, 78
Isabella, Archduchess of Austria, 8
Isebrande, Marion, 6–7
Italians, 104
Italy, 19

James, Saint, 88
James I, King of England (King of Scotland as James VI), 118, 122, 127, 131, 132–33
James III, King of Scotland, 122
James IV, King of Scotland, 124–25
James V, King of Scotland, 123, 127
James VI, King of Scotland. *See* James I, King of England
Jerusalem, 124–25
John I, King of England: in "Description of England," 60; in "Historie of England," 1577 edition, 26, 30, 32; in "Historie of England," 1587 edition, 39, 40–41; in "Historie of Ireland," 1577 edition, 90

John of Fordun, 119
Joseph of Arimathea, 2, 31
Jure apud Scotos, De (Buchanan), 118

Kanicus, 81
Kenelm, 24
Kenneth II, King of Scotland, 121
Kile, 109
Kilkenny, Statutes of, 79
Killigrew, Henry, 51
King John (Shakespeare), 136, 141
King Lear (Shakespeare), 136, 141
Kingsford, C. L., 142
Kinney, Arthur, 142
Knox, John, 127

Lambard, William, 10, 56
Lan, Richard, 138
Latimer, Hugh, 6
League of Friendship, 133
Leinster, 77, 87, 104
Leland, John, 4–5; and *Chronicles*'s financing, 17; and "Description of England," 56, 57, 72–73; and "Historie of England," 1577 edition, 35; and "Historie of Scotland," 1577 edition, 116
Leslie, John, *De Origine Moribus et Rebus Gestis Scotorum*, 16, 126, 127, 128, 129, 130
Levy, F. J., 136, 142
Lhuyd, Humfrey, 116–17, 129
Lillo, George, 136
"Lives of the Archbishops of Canterbury, The" (Thynne), 16, 51
London, 10, 11
Lyly, John, 136

Macbeth (Shakespeare), 116, 120, 136, 144
Macbeth, King of Scotland, 116, 120–21
Macbeth, Lady, 120
Macduff, 120
MacTeige, Sir Cormac, 106
Major, John, 116, 122, 124, 128
Malcolm, King of Scotland, 120
Maldwin, King of Scotland, 119
Margan, 24

The Author

Alison Taufer is an associate professor of English at California State University, Los Angeles. She received her undergraduate education at Loyola Marymount University and pursued graduate studies at the University of California, Los Angeles, where she received a Ph.D. in comparative literature in 1988. She has published articles and reviews on English and Spanish sixteenth-century literature and on Asian-American literature.

The Editor

Arthur F. Kinney is the Thomas W. Copeland Professor of Literary History at the University of Massachusetts, Amherst, and the Director of the Center for Renaissance Studies there; he is also an adjunct professor of English at New York University. He has written several books in the field: *Humanist Poetics, Continental Humanist Poetics, John Skelton: Priest as Poet,* and the forthcoming *Lies Like the Truth: 'Macbeth' and the Cultural Moment* are among them. He is the founding editor of the journal *English Literary Renaissance* and editor of the book series "Massachusetts Studies in Early Modern Culture."